Dan Good

HarperCollins
LEADERSHIP

AN IMPRINT OF HarperCollins

T0104387

THE
MICROSOFT
STORY

How the Tech Giant Rebooted Its Culture,
Upgraded Its Strategy, and Found Success
in the Cloud

Published by HarperCollins Leadership, an imprint of HarperCollins Focus LLC.

Published in association with Kevin Anderson & Associates: https://www.ka-writing.com/.

Book design by Aubrey Khan, Neuwirth & Associates.

ISBN 978-1-4002-2391-6 (eBook)
ISBN 978-1-4002-2390-9 (HC)

Library of Congress Control Number: 2020941845

Printed in the United States of America
20 21 22 23 LSC 10 9 8 7 6 5 4 3 2 1

CONTENTS

Contents

ACKNOWLEDGMENTS

Writing a book is a solitary and collaborative process, all at the same time. I'm grateful for the chance to speak with Mario Juarez, who spent decades as a communications leader at Microsoft; Nathan Myhrvold, formerly Microsoft's chief technology officer; Microsoft Chief Storyteller Steve Clayton; and longtime tech and video game journalist Dean Takahashi—your insights were so helpful to me.

Thanks goes to HarperCollins and Kevin Anderson & Associates for the opportunity to write about such a fascinating company.

I'm forever grateful to those who've helped me along the way, especially my parents.

To Suzy and Dean, your love and support mean the world to me.

Dan

1975
Bill Gates and Paul Allen receive a contract to write a BASIC interpreter for Altair, and they start Micro-Soft.

1979
Microsoft's BASIC interpreter becomes the first microprocessor software product to surpass $1 million in sales.

1983
Allen resigns from Microsoft. The first version of Microsoft Word is released.

1985
The first version of Windows is released, as well as Word 2.0.

1986
Microsoft goes public and is first traded at $25.50 a share.

1996
Microsoft releases its first smartphone, the Windows CE. Microsoft-backed network MSNBC launches.

2000
Gates is replaced by longtime executive Steve Ballmer as CEO. Gates stays on as chairman and chief software architect.

2020

Microsoft rises to $185 a share, entering a virtual tie with Apple as the world's most valuable company.

1,000,000,000,000

2019

The company reaches a $1 trillion market cap, joining Apple and Amazon.

2016

Microsoft acquires LinkedIn for $26.2 billion and joins the Linux Foundation.

2014

Satya Nadella becomes the third CEO in Microsoft's history.

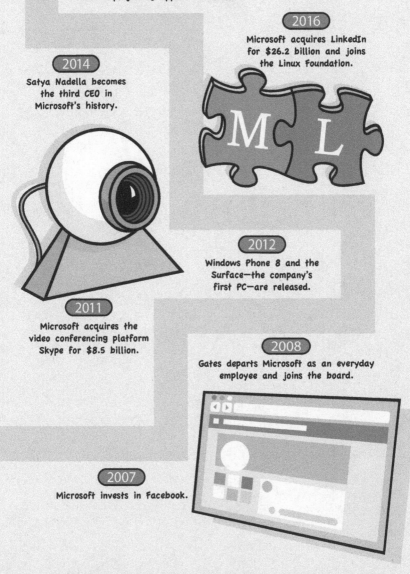

2012

Windows Phone 8 and the Surface—the company's first PC—are released.

2011

Microsoft acquires the video conferencing platform Skype for $8.5 billion.

2008

Gates departs Microsoft as an everyday employee and joins the board.

2007

Microsoft invests in Facebook.

Microsoft isn't cool. The company, founded in 1975, has a reputation for humdrum business-oriented products and capitalizing on market advantages. It didn't develop its own desktop personal computers or invent the first word processors, spreadsheets, or graphical user interfaces. It wasn't the first company to create an internet browser or email service or video game system, and was surpassed in mobile phones and search engines and cloud technology and social media.

And yet, Microsoft finds itself one of the greatest business success stories in United States history—a global tech giant with its own line of PCs in the Surface; and "killer apps" with Microsoft Word and Excel; and its benchmark interface, Windows; and the Internet Explorer browser; and the Outlook email platform; and Xbox for video games; and the Bing search engine; and Microsoft Azure cloud technology; and LinkedIn for social media. The 148,000-employee Microsoft was worth nearly $1.4 trillion in early 2020, neck and neck with Apple for the world's most valuable company. But beyond market value, its impact can be measured in the ability to empower people and businesses to fulfill their purpose and achieve more.

Which makes Microsoft pretty damn cool, after all.

In the pages that follow, we will take a deeper look at the story of Microsoft, charting its creation by two childhood friends to its rise into one of the world's most successful—and yes, coolest—companies.

> " Microsoft finds itself one of the greatest business success stories in United States history—a global tech giant with its own line of PCs in the Surface; and "killer apps" with Microsoft Word and Excel; and its benchmark interface, Windows; and the Internet Explorer browser; and the Outlook email platform; and Xbox for video games; and the Bing search engine; and Microsoft Azure cloud technology; and LinkedIn for social media.

THE
MICROSOFT
STORY

"I was a sponge, soaking up knowledge wherever I could. All of us were sponges then."

—PAUL ALLEN,
Cofounder of Microsoft

THE MICROSOFT STORY

CHAPTER ONE

THE EARLY YEARS

The future was here. Paul Allen rushed through Harvard Square to reach his friend Bill Gates to show him the January 1975 issue of *Popular Electronics,* the magazine devoted to gadgets and gizmos.

The gizmo on the cover would change computers forever—and inspire the creation of one of the world's most influential companies.

World's First Minicomputer Kit to Rival Commercial Models . . .
"Altair 8800"

The article about the Altair 8800 picked up on page thirty-three.

The era of the computer in every home—a favorite topic among science-fiction writers—has arrived! It's made possible by the POPULAR ELECTRONICS/MITS Altair 8800, a full-blown computer that can hold its own against sophisticated minicomputers now on the market. And it doesn't cost several thousand dollars. In fact, it's in a color TV-receiver's price class—under $400 for a complete kit.

The Altair 8800 is not a "demonstrator" or souped-up calculator. It is the most powerful computer ever presented as a construction project in any electronics magazine. In many ways, it represents a revolutionary development in electronic design and thinking.[1]

The computer's front panel included rows of switches and LEDs. Behind the lid, the Altair featured an 8-bit parallel processor and 65,000 words of maximum memory, along with a new LSI chip and seventy-eight basic machine instructions (as compared with forty in the usual minicomputer). "This means that you can write an extensive and detailed program," the authors wrote.[2] But someone would have to write that program. Allen and Gates thought they might be the people to do it. The pair had been teaming up ever since their days at the Lakeside School, a private boys' school in Washington State. Allen, a multifaceted dreamer, was born in 1953. Gates, a bookish, driven pragmatist, came along two years later. They both were drawn to computers and coding while attending the Lakeside School.[3] At the time, computers were massive and clunky and expensive and exclusive, generally only available to government agencies or major companies or academics in math and science disciplines.

Lakeside had a Teletype Model ASR-33 (for Automatic Send and Receive) terminal with a paper tape reader that linked over the school's phone line to a GE-635, "a General Electric mainframe computer in a distant, unknown office," Allen recalled decades later.

"The Teletype made a terrific racket, a mix of low humming, the Gatling gun of the paper-tape punch, and the *ka-chacko-whack* of the printer keys. The room's walls and ceiling had to be lined with white corkboard for soundproofing. But though it was noisy and slow, a dumb remote terminal with no display screen or lower-case letters, the ASR-33 was also state-of-the-art. I was transfixed. I sensed that you could do things with this machine."[4]

The school's Mothers Club held a rummage sale and used the proceeds to buy the Teletype and computer time on the GE computer. But computer time was expensive—whoever was using it had to be efficient and creative. "You would type the programs off-line on this yellow paper tape and then put it into the tape reader, dial up the computer, and very quickly feed in the paper tape and run your program," Gates said. "They charged you not only for the connect time, but also for storage units and CPU time. So, if you had a program that had a loop in it of some type you could spend a lot of money very quickly. And so we went through the money that the Mothers Club had given very rapidly. It was a little awkward for the teachers, because it was just students sitting there and zoom—the money was gone."[5]

The system used a computer language called BASIC that was developed in 1964 by Dartmouth College math professors John Kemeny and Thomas Kurtz (BASIC, speaking to its ambitions for widespread use, stands for Beginners' All-purpose Symbolic Instruction Code).[6] Computers needed language to run, and even if computers weren't readily available for public use, BASIC created the potential of computer programming for the masses.

Allen and Gates Meet

It was in that Teletype room, amid the Gatling gun of the paper-tape punch and *ka-chacko-whack* of the printer keys, that Paul Allen and Bill Gates first connected. The pair reflected an image of contrasts. The older Allen, with his long side-burns and stocky build, looked a decade older than the boy-ish, gaunt Gates.

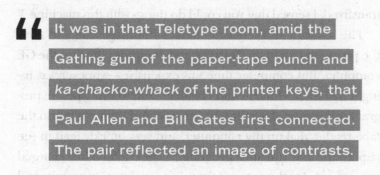

It was in that Teletype room, amid the Gatling gun of the paper-tape punch and *ka-chacko-whack* of the printer keys, that Paul Allen and Bill Gates first connected. The pair reflected an image of contrasts.

Where Allen's family struggled to afford tuition but wanted to challenge him (his father was a University of Washington librarian and his mother was a schoolteacher),[7] Gates, nicknamed "Trey" as a child, had been raised in a prominent family—his father was a successful lawyer and his mother was involved with the boards of nonprofits.[8]

Despite all of their differences, they also had many similarities. They both were drawn to the limitless potential of computers and felt like a wave of opportunity was approaching. Companies such as Hewlett-Packard and Intel Corporation were emerging, and developments in memory storage and word processing were on the horizon.

Something big was happening. And Allen and Gates wanted to be a part of it.

The Lakeside Programming Group

Gates and Allen joined two other students—Ric Weiland and Kent Evans—as the most consistent visitors to the computer room. The older Allen and Weiland often paired up together, and the younger Gates and Evans quickly became best friends, reading business magazines and planning their future companies.

"We were always creating funny company names and having people send us their product literature," Gates said. "Trying to think about how business worked. And in particular, looking at computer companies and what was going on with them."[9]

As the group kept burning through the Mothers Club's computer budget, a new opportunity emerged—a time-sharing company called the Computer Center Corporation, or C-Cubed, opened in Seattle and needed testers for its Digital Equipment Corporation PDP-10 computer, since its TOPS-10 operating system was known to crash.[10]

C-Cubed offered the teens unlimited free time as testers on the company's terminals. There, they began studying code and mastering different machine language such as BASIC, COBOL (Common Business-Oriented Language), and FORTRAN (Formula Translation). Computer pioneers at C-Cubed would loan Gates and the other teens system manuals and teach them about assembly code in drips and drabs. Other times, Allen and Gates would go dumpster diving through the trash to find discarded operating system listings. Gates's weight made it easier for Allen to propel him.

"It was so exciting to get a little glimpse and beginning to figure out how computers were built, and why they were expensive," Gates recalled decades later. "I certainly think that having some dimension, when you're young, that you feel a mastery of, versus the other people around you is a very positive thing."[11]

After testing of the PDP-10 was completed, C-Cubed began charging the teens for computer time. One month, Allen's charge came to $78, which would amount to more than $500 in 2019. "I know you're learning, but can't you cut back?" his father asked him.[12]

Gates and Allen tried to tap into C-Cubed's internal files in hopes of finding a free account. Instead, they got caught, and they lost their C-Cubed privileges for the summer. That fall, Allen—in exchange for free computer time—was tasked with trying to improve C-Cubed's BASIC compiler, a program that translates source code.[13]

Allen pored through the assembly code "like an apprentice watchmaker squinting at the tiny wheels to understand their interplay," he wrote, piecing the code together word by word and becoming a BASIC virtuoso.[14]

C-Cubed taught the boys another lesson in 1970 when it closed. The company never established a solid business model. There was money to be made through computers, but you couldn't fund a company on the strength of free computer time.

With C-Cubed closed, the teens branched out. Allen, then a high school senior, began spending his time at the University of Washington's graduate computer science lab. "I was a sponge, soaking up knowledge wherever I could," he said.[15] "All of us were sponges then."

That fall, a time-sharing company in Portland hired Allen and his three "colleagues"—Gates, Weiland, and Evans—to write a payroll program in COBOL, the high-level language, and the Lakeside Programming Group was born.

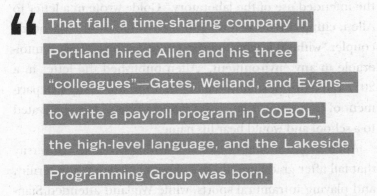

> That fall, a time-sharing company in Portland hired Allen and his three "colleagues"—Gates, Weiland, and Evans—to write a payroll program in COBOL, the high-level language, and the Lakeside Programming Group was born.

The project was sprawling and cumbersome. Evans and Gates did much of the heavy lifting, but after Allen and Weiland worried there wouldn't be enough work to go around, the upperclassmen decided they could take on the project alone.

"I'm sure their friends thought it was weird that we were coming around at all, and then they decide they just want to do it. So they kicked both Kent and I off the project," Gates said. "And I said, 'I think you're underestimating how hard this is. If you ask me to come back, I am going to be totally in charge of this and anything you ever asked me to do again.'"[16]

Soon enough, Allen was asking Gates to rejoin the project, and just as he said, Gates took ownership. "It was just more natural for me to be in charge," he said.

Gates had an innate ability to synthesize information quickly. When confronted with a situation, he'd rock forward and backward, forward and backward in his chair, a means of focusing and centering himself. But Gates's analytical mind couldn't help his friends secure computer access.

In March 1971, computer lab director Dr. Hellmut Golde kicked Allen and his high school friends out of the lab. Their work "has caused a number of complaints and tends to disrupt the intended use of the laboratory," Golde wrote in a letter to Allen, citing the noise level and their removal of an acoustic coupler "without leaving at least a note. Such behavior is intolerable in any environment." Allen published the letter in a 2017 LinkedIn post announcing that the university's Department of Computer Science & Engineering was being elevated to a school and would bear his name.[17]

Allen began taking classes at Washington State University that fall after graduating from Lakeside, pledging a fraternity, and playing intramural sports, while Weiland attended Stanford, majoring in electrical engineering. The youngest members of the Lakeside Programming Group, meanwhile, were tasked with solving a new problem. Their school had merged with a local all-girls school, and Lakeside's principal needed a program to organize the class schedules.

But in May of 1972, before they could begin the project, tragedy struck. Kent Evans, Gates's closest friend, was taking a mountaineering class when he slipped and fell down a slope and died. He was seventeen years old.

"It was so unexpected, so unusual," Gates said.[18]

A Strong Pair

A grieving Gates asked Allen to help him with the scheduling program, and the friends fell into a routine, working around the clock, sleeping on cots, and going to the movies for breaks.

"I was impressed by how cleanly Bill broke the job into its component parts, and especially how he 'preloaded' himself into an English class with a dozen or more girls and no other boys," Allen wrote in his memoir, *Idea Man*. "Bill and I became closer that summer. Our age gap no longer seemed to matter; we had what I call high-bandwidth communication."[19]

That high-bandwidth communication continued with their next opportunity, which involved data processing about traffic flow—Gates called the program Traf-O-Data, playing off of the term jack-o'-lantern.[20]

Allen was drawn to the potential of the microprocessor, the heart of the computer. A colleague, Paul Gilbert, helped build a machine around an Intel 8-bit 8008 microprocessor.

The pair were also enlisted for early 1973, Gates's final semester in high school, to work on a complicated software project through the aerospace company TRW that involved a PDP-10 mainframe computer.[21] Allen took a leave of absence from Washington State, while Gates received approval for a senior project. They were paid $4 an hour and worked for days at a time.

The friends didn't spend too much time sleeping. Gates, when needing an energy rush, would pour the orange powder Tang into his hand and lick it, leaving his face and hands (and computer keys) covered in orange residue.[22] As Gates was licking Tang out of his palm and working on the TRW project, he received his acceptance to Harvard University. So off to Boston he went, three thousand miles away from home and his coding cohort.

Allen and Gates talked about leaving school and starting a company, "but it was too vague and my parents wanted me to go back to school," Gates said.[23] But the conversation never really went away. They eventually started getting clients for their traffic data collection—Traf-O-Data was finally taking off! But when Washington started offering similar services to cities for free, Traf-O-Data was pretty much finished.

Gates kept suggesting that Allen should move to Boston, so Allen inquired at different companies and ended up getting a job offer from Honeywell, the engineering and aerospace company. Gates received a job offer there, too.

"Then, after I accepted the job and prepared to take another leave from Wazzu [a nickname for Washington State University], Bill changed his mind and decided to go back to Harvard," Allen wrote. "I suspected heavy pressure from his parents, who had more traditional ideas."[24]

Either way, Allen was making a move. He and his girlfriend, Rita, drove to Boston. Allen and Gates were together again.

Honeywell wasn't what Allen expected—"a big cocoon where people punched the clock as though they were working for the phone company." Bored with the job, Allen used his friend's password to hack into Harvard's operating system, Unix.

Eventually, Rita had to return to Washington and Allen was stuck in a stale job, struggling to find his next project. He'd come up with ideas and bring them up to Gates, but the technology wasn't adequate.

It would stay that way until the friends saw the Altair 8800 on the cover of *Popular Electronics*. And then they sprang into action.

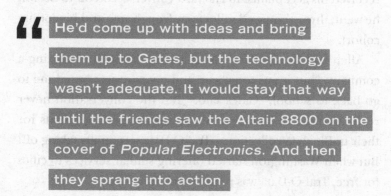

❝ He'd come up with ideas and bring them up to Gates, but the technology wasn't adequate. It would stay that way until the friends saw the Altair 8800 on the cover of *Popular Electronics*. And then they sprang into action.

Calling Their Shot

On January 2, 1975, Allen mailed a letter to MITS, or Micro Instrumentation and Telemetry Systems, the company behind the Altair 8800. "We have available a BASIC language interpreter which runs on MCS-8080 series microcomputers," Allen wrote. "We are interested in selling copies of this software to hobbyists thru you. It could be supplied on cassettes or floppy disks to users of your ALTAIR series microcomputers. We would anticipate charging you $50 a copy which you would then sell for somewhere between $75 and $100. If you are interested, please contact us."[25] They sent the letter on letterhead from Traf-O-Data, their defunct traffic data collection company.

MITS employees did not respond to the letter, so Gates called MITS, and the pair got to work. They faced multiple obstacles. Most notably, they'd be creating the interpreter without using an Altair or Intel 8080 microprocessor.

But Allen and Gates had a head start because of their work with Traf-O-Data, and they were savvy enough to recognize that they were onto something special. They saw a problem, an opportunity, a need—who else would be better suited than them? And they believed in their ability to find an answer.

Their biggest concern involved floating-point math code and the need for decimals to be in the right places in their code. As they discussed the issue at a Harvard cafeteria, a nearby student, Monte Davidoff, spoke up. "I've done those for the PDP-8," said Davidoff, who became a third member of the team.[26]

Gates handled the interpreter's programming while Davidoff tackled the math package. The team regularly pulled all-nighters, motivating and inspiring one another, driving each other to achieve something beyond themselves. "We worked all hours, with double shifts on weekends. Bill basically stopped going to class," Allen remembered.[27]

About eight weeks and 3,200 bytes later, the interpreter was complete. It was time to test their work for MITS. If the interpreter worked, the contract would be theirs. If it failed, well, they tried not to focus on that possibility. Bill Gates checked and rechecked Paul Allen's work. It appeared to be correct.

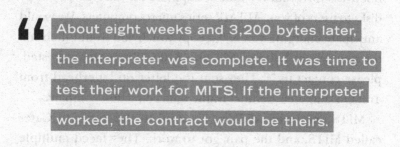

> **About eight weeks and 3,200 bytes later, the interpreter was complete. It was time to test their work for MITS. If the interpreter worked, the contract would be theirs.**

Allen packed the paper tape and flew to Albuquerque to meet with MITS. Two months of work, research, and planning on a roll of paper. During the flight, Allen realized they'd forgotten something important—a bootstrap loader. The sequence of instructions was necessary in order for the interpreter to run. "Without one, that yellow tape in my briefcase would be worthless," Allen said.[28]

So, Allen scrawled loader code on a steno pad and hoped for the best. The next day, Allen worked with the Altair for the first time, toggling the switches on the front panel. *This isn't going to work,* he thought. He pressed the RUN switch, and the processor executed the steps. OK, one step down. *But this isn't going to work . . .*

Now it was time for the Teletype to read the paper tape, which took seven minutes.

At the end, the printer produced two words. MEMORY SIZE? "7168," Allen typed.

"OK," the printer responded.

Allen typed a command—the moment of truth.

"PRINT 2+2."

"4," the machine responded.

It worked! They'd solved the problem. The contract was theirs. Pretty soon, Allen was moving to New Mexico to serve as MITS's director of software development.

The first issue of *Computer Notes*, a newsletter for Altair users, published on April 7, 1975, heralded the group's achievement on its cover under the headline **ALTAIR BASIC—UP AND RUNNING**.

"There are two keys to the new computer revolution. One is computers must be inexpensive and the other is computers must be understandable. With the Altair 8800 and Altair BASIC, both of these criteria have been met," editor David Bunnell wrote.[29]

The names Paul Allen and Bill Gates weren't anywhere in the story, and that was completely fine for the young programmers. "Our relationship was perfectly symbiotic," Allen recalled in *Idea Man*.[30] "Bill and I benefited from [MIT founder Ed Roberts's] distribution and marketing networks, while MITS, a classic early innovator, got out front with our programmer-friendly language and dedicated support and upgrades."

At the end of the spring semester, Gates and Monte Davidoff joined Allen in New Mexico, and soon after, a younger Lakeside student, Chris Larson, followed. Eventually, Gates and Allen had a lawyer write up a contract for the 8080 BASIC, and MITS's Roberts signed off without reading it. They'd seized their moment.

But what to name their partnership? Allen had an idea for their company name: Microprocessors and Software—MicroSoft. The name had a nice ring to it.

Micro-Soft.

Sending a Message

Despite all of the young programmers' success, by the end of 1975, their royalties for the BASIC were only $16,005,[31] mainly because most users were getting their BASIC software for free and regularly sharing bootleg copies.

It was the model set forth by groups like California's Homebrew Computer Club, which shared bootleg copies of software and viewed computers not as a commercial enterprise, but a collegial one (among its members were Steve Jobs and Steve Wozniak, the founders of Apple).

Bill Gates fumed. It was time to take a stand and protect his company's creative property. So Gates, all of twenty years old, penned his full-throated statement of purpose to the computer world, "An Open Letter to the Hobby." This was Gates's 95 Theses nailed to the church door.

" So Gates, all of twenty years old, penned his full-throated statement of purpose to the computer world, "An Open Letter to the Hobby." This was Gates's 95 Theses nailed to the church door.

As the majority of hobbyists must be aware, most of you steal your software. Hardware must be paid for, but software is something to share. Who cares if the people who worked on it get paid? Is this fair?

Who can afford to do professional work for nothing? What hobbyist can put 3-man years into programming, finding all the bugs, documenting his product and distribute it for free?

We have written 6800 BASIC, and are writing 8080 APL and 6800 APL, but there is very little incentive to make this software available to hobbyists. Most directly, the thing you do is theft.

Nothing would please me more than being able to hire ten programmers and deluge the hobby market with good software.

Bill Gates
General Partner
Micro-Soft[32]

The letter infuriated the industry and created friction between Gates and MITS founder Ed Roberts. *Who did this pompous college kid think he was?*

Gates's letter was a harbinger of things to come, establishing Microsoft's marching orders and hinting at the changing tides of the computer world. While Altair had a head start, other companies caught up and started offering similar products. And the market trends were a clarion call for Gates and Allen, who started licensing BASIC for other companies, with money from each deal going back to MITS. The goal for Micro-Soft: "to provide all language software for every microcomputer on the market," Allen said.

Within a few years, the company's goals would galvanize around a central theme: "A computer on every desk, and in every home, running Microsoft software."[33]

By late 1976, Allen quit MITS and focused exclusively on Micro-Soft. The company moved into its first office in Albuquerque and added its earliest employees: Marc McDonald, another former Lakeside student; their old Lakeside friend Ric Weiland; Steve Wood; and Chris Larson.

And Bill Gates, against his parents' wishes, was ready to quit Harvard.

Gates and Allen (OK, Gates) struggled to quantify their share of the company. Gates initially requested a 60-40 split of proceeds, but he later suggested a 64-36 cut because he was doing more of the work on BASIC.

"His intellectual horsepower had been critical to BASIC, and he would be central to our success moving forward. That much was obvious," Allen wrote years later.[34] "But how to calculate the value of my Big Idea—the mating of a high-level language with a microprocessor—or my persistence in bringing Bill to see it?"

Allen didn't care to fight. What was a few points? What was a few hundred thousand, a few million, a few billion? Allen agreed to Gates's suggestions and hoped the conversation was behind them. The pair signed a formal partnership agreement on February 3, 1977, that included a clause in the event of "irreconcilable differences," in which Gates could demand Allen's withdrawl.

But that was the furthest thing from Allen's mind at the time, especially as the personal computer landscape continued to change. The Commodore PET, TandyTRS-80, Apple II, and Trinity were all reaching the market (Apple licensed Microsoft's 12K BASIC interpreter and called it Applesoft).

As MITS continued to lose market share, Ed Roberts decided to sell the company to Pertec Computer Corporation—along with the rights to Microsoft's BASIC. After Allen and

Gates threatened to terminate their contract with MITS, MITS and Pertec filed for arbitration, and amid the legal battle, Microsoft was barred from any new BASIC contracts.[35]

It was a crisis point. Microsoft, brought to a standstill, struggled to pay its bills and make payroll. If Microsoft lost, it could spell the end of the company, or at the very least, their licensing model.

Allen thought Microsoft should settle. Gates disagreed. After seven months of court hearings and paperwork and doubt, the arbitrator ruled in Microsoft's favor, freeing the company from its MITS contract and forcing Pertec to pay Microsoft royalty fees.

"Most crucially, Bill and I recovered all rights to our BASIC interpreter and could now sell it to whomever we pleased—and better yet, keep all the revenue. Our one big roadblock was gone," Allen said.[36] The contracts for Microsoft's BASIC poured in, and Microsoft received licenses for the Commodore PET and TRS-80 computers.

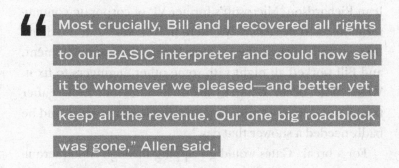

Most crucially, Bill and I recovered all rights to our BASIC interpreter and could now sell it to whomever we pleased—and better yet, keep all the revenue. Our one big roadblock was gone," Allen said.

Push It to the Limit

As the company's popularity exploded, Gates's demanding, demeaning style motivated and grated on the employees, most notably Allen. He was known to push staffers beyond their breaking point—"that is the stupidest thing I've ever heard," he'd grouse—or study license plates in the parking lot on weekends, expecting others to be as devoted to Microsoft as he was. Even though Allen had issues with Gates's bedside manners, he never doubted his conviction.

Gates "could be callous and rude, but he had a warmer, human side, too," Allen remembered. "And no one doubted that his excesses, for good or ill, were spontaneous. When Bill blew his stack at a meeting, it was never merely for effect."[37]

Gates would work for days at a time—he was too distracted or busy to worry about personal hygiene and take a shower. Sometimes his secretary would arrive to work to find him passed out on the ground, exhausted.

"If he was busy he didn't bathe, he didn't change clothes," Jean Richardson, Microsoft's former VP of corporate communications, said in 1995.[38] "We were in New York and the demo that we had crashed the evening before the announcement, and Bill worked all night with some other engineers to fix it. Well it didn't occur to him to take 10 minutes for a shower after that, it just didn't occur to him that that was important, and he badly needed a shower that day."

For a break, Gates would go zipping through Albuquerque and racing into the desert to blow off steam. On one such joyride, on December 13, 1977, Gates was pulled over and taken into custody. The mug shot is part of Microsoft's lore, showing Gates, all of twenty-two years old, wearing a floral print shirt and blue sweater, his hair a mop of straw over his ears, posing for police with a smile on his face.[39]

The mug shot was one of the famous images from Microsoft's early years. Another iconic photo shows eleven of Microsoft's earliest employees posing together for a portrait in 1978, amid a snowstorm—Bob Greenberg won a free portrait from a radio giveaway.[40] The family photo hints at something deeper, a bond forged in 1970s counterculture that would soon bleed into America's mainstream. Computers weren't *cool* in the 1970s. But they soon would be.

> Another iconic photo shows eleven of Microsoft's earliest employees posing together for a portrait in 1978, amid a snowstorm—Bob Greenberg won a free portrait from a radio giveaway. The family photo hints at something deeper, a bond forged in 1970s counterculture that would soon bleed into America's mainstream.

Paul Allen has his scraggly beard. Bill Gates still looks like he's in high school. The hair and sideburns were as big as the group's dreams, and the clothes were as 1970s as shag carpeting. The twentysomethings were ready to rule the world, no matter what you thought of their style.

But they couldn't rule the computer world in Albuquerque, which was about a thousand miles away from California's Silicon Valley, the country's emerging tech hub, where the IBMs and Apples had grown roots.

MITS, which had been sold to Pertec, was no longer keeping Microsoft in Albuquerque, Microsoft's founders weren't from New Mexico, and most significantly, Gates and Allen were homesick.

Moving Microsoft to the Emerald City would position it a short plane flight away from Silicon Valley and allow its founders to settle in their hometown—local boys who made good.

So, in 1979, the year Microsoft's BASIC interpreter became the first microprocessor software product to surpass $1 million in sales,[41] the company moved to the Seattle suburb of Bellevue, Washington. Gates and Allen were back home, and they'd come a long way from Traf-O-Data and C-Cubed and the Lakeside computer room.

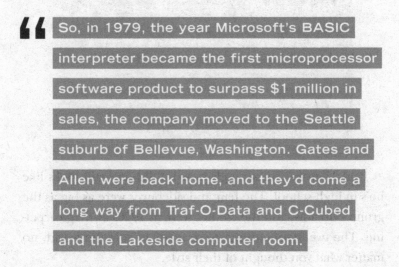

So, in 1979, the year Microsoft's BASIC interpreter became the first microprocessor software product to surpass $1 million in sales, the company moved to the Seattle suburb of Bellevue, Washington. Gates and Allen were back home, and they'd come a long way from Traf-O-Data and C-Cubed and the Lakeside computer room.

Growth and Attention

Microsoft's growth wasn't contained to the Pacific Northwest. Allen and Gates traveled to Japan in August 1979 to meet with Kazuhiko (Kay) Nishi, a Microsoft agent and magazine publisher, and the company opened its first international offices, known as ASCII Microsoft (later Microsoft Japan). Other offices would emerge across the globe in the ensuing years.

As Microsoft picked up steam, so did offers from prospective buyers. One such inquiry came from a Texas billionaire, H. Ross Perot, who founded the data processing service company Electronic Data Systems and later made runs for president in 1992 and 1996. Perot was interested in buying Microsoft. But Gates wasn't ready to sell. "At present we wish to remain independent," Gates wrote in response. "We see the potential to double the size of our organization and earn over $2 million per year before taxes."[42]

Microsoft ended up bringing in $2.4 million in revenue in 1979.

But Microsoft was still finding its way and trying to separate itself amid the PC arms race. The companies were all looking for the next big thing—easy-to-use software that could draw in non-computer users.

Dan Bricklin and colleague Bob Frankston found that next big thing. Bricklin, a Harvard grad student, imagined "an electronic blackboard" in which a user could input values and the computer would spit out solutions.[43] He arranged his blackboard using a grid pattern, with rows numbered 1, 2, 3 going down the left side of the screen and columns—A, B, C, D—from left to right to create the first computer spreadsheet program.

The program, originally by Personal Software, was called VisiCalc—standing for "visible calculator"—and it ran on the

Apple II computer. Personal Software considered pursuing a patent for the electronic blackboard but didn't think their effort would be successful. "If I invented the spreadsheet today, of course I would file for a patent," Bricklin wrote. "That's the law of the land . . . today. The companies I have been involved with since Software Arts have filed for patents on many of their inventions. In 1979, almost nobody tried to patent software inventions."[44]

When Paul Allen saw VisiCalc for the first time at the 1979 National Computer Conference, it confirmed his (and Gates's) belief that a computer's software—the programs running on the computer—were more important than the hardware itself. "We hadn't counted on someone outflanking us with a whole new approach," Allen recalled.[45]

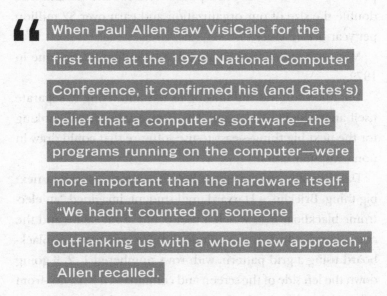

When Paul Allen saw VisiCalc for the first time at the 1979 National Computer Conference, it confirmed his (and Gates's) belief that a computer's software—the programs running on the computer—were more important than the hardware itself. "We hadn't counted on someone outflanking us with a whole new approach," Allen recalled.

Microsoft in the applications business?
Hmmm . . .

Employee No. 30

Steve Ballmer was not someone you easily ignored. Loud, brilliant, and brash, Ballmer befriended Gates at Harvard, and at his buddy's urging, moved to Washington in 1980 to help run Microsoft's business operations.

Ballmer was the kind of guy who'd challenge Gates and keep him on his toes while remaining loyal to him. Ballmer grew up in the Detroit suburbs and also spent three years of his childhood living in Brussels—his father was a manager at Ford Motor Company.[46] A math whiz, Ballmer scored an 800 on his SAT in math. He graduated from Harvard and spent two years working at Procter & Gamble before becoming Microsoft's thirtieth employee.

Ballmer was Microsoft's first legitimate business manager— and his arrival changed the dynamic between Allen and Gates, shifting it to a triumvirate. Gates, in fact, used a bit of trickery to hire Ballmer. After Allen and Gates agreed to offer Ballmer up to 5 percent of the company, Gates turned around and offered Ballmer 8.75 percent and didn't tell Allen—the cofounder was actually on vacation at the time. Allen later said he found out the truth from reading a company memo.[47] He confronted Gates, and Gates told Allen that he would cover the difference with his own share of the company.

Gates was shrewd about bringing in the people he needed to build his company, and if there was any doubt, the hiring of Ballmer cemented Microsoft as Bill Gates's company.

Gates, in a 1993 interview, acknowledged friction with Allen—but stressed Ballmer's deep impact in helping the company mature. "Even though I was running the business, it was a partnership. [Allen's] role was very, very critical to so many of the transitions that we made. There was always some strain because I was pushing people to work hard, including Paul," Gates said.

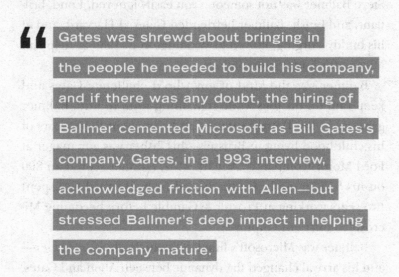

> Gates was shrewd about bringing in the people he needed to build his company, and if there was any doubt, the hiring of Ballmer cemented Microsoft as Bill Gates's company. Gates, in a 1993 interview, acknowledged friction with Allen—but stressed Ballmer's deep impact in helping the company mature.

"When Steve came in, I was spending more time with him because the business side was important; managing and organizing, and [deciding] what we were going to do about international. So, it was great that Steve was smart enough and personal enough, that even though he didn't have a technical background, the programmers accepted him."

A New Decade

Microsoft, which built its early success with computer language, entered the 1980s looking to make a splash with operating systems. It reached a deal to license a version of AT&T's Unix, named XENIX, in 1980. Unix was popular with programmers, academic institutions, and large companies due to its multi-user capabilities. But it also took lots of memory, making it difficult for early PCs to run Unix.

The Unix philosophy valued a collection of individual programs doing individual tasks—and out of Unix would eventually come Linux, an open-source operating system that could be used across various hardware.

After reaching the deal for XENIX, Microsoft found itself collaborating with a rival of AT&T—a partnership that would send XENIX to the background but cement Microsoft as the upstart computer company of the 1980s.

"In some ways, it was the stars just perfectly aligning. But let's be really, really clear about the bright star in the middle, which was Bill Gates."

—MARIO JUAREZ,
Former Senior Communications Leader at Microsoft

CHAPTER TWO

LIFTOFF

Bill Gates's mother, Mary, was his biggest cheerleader. It was a nice change of pace from his teenage days, when they consistently clashed. He wanted to sit in his room and read, while Mary, a social butterfly who served on numerous charity boards, urged Bill to see the outside world and develop benevolence.[1]

Son and mother strengthened their relationship as the years passed, and Mary Gates was proud of Bill's accomplishments, regularly singing his praises to anyone who would listen. She was serving on the national United Way committee alongside John Opel, then chairman of IBM Corp., in 1980 when she discussed her son's company to Opel.[2]

Opel, as the story goes, mentioned the conversation to IBM execs, who were considering different companies to create an operating system for its computer. IBM was on an escalated timeline, so it would need to export key responsibilities. After Mary Gates's conversation, Microsoft got a foot in the door, but it would be up to Gates and Microsoft to seal the deal. IBM exec Jack Sams arrived at Microsoft's offices with other company leaders, and this "young fella" came out to greet them.

"I thought he was the office boy," Sams said. The "office boy" turned out to be Gates.[3]

IBM's team produced a nondisclosure agreement about "Project Chess"—the code name for IBM's PC—and Gates signed it. But as IBM's execs spoke to Gates and Ballmer, they realized Microsoft didn't have any experience with operating systems.

Gates mentioned Gary Kildall, who was responsible for the first operating system on the PC and ran a company called Digital Research. Kildall was the industry's leader in operating systems, the creator of CP/M, or Control Program for Microcomputers, while Microsoft had focused on interpreters and computer language.

Gates called Kildall with IBM in the room. "Gary, I'm sending some guys down. They're going to be on the phone. Treat them right, they're important guys," Gates said.[4]

The IBM execs visited the California headquarters of Digital Research, which was run by Kildall and his wife, Dorothy. When IBM produced the same NDA it had given to Gates, Dorothy Kildall deferred to the company's lawyer and kept IBM waiting. Digital Research and IBM struggled to get on the same page.[5]

Eventually, IBM returned to Microsoft. "Digital Research didn't seize that, and we knew it was essential, if somebody didn't do it, the project was going to fall apart," Gates said in 1995.

Microsoft was in line for the IBM contract, but there was a catch—it still didn't have an operating system ready. Luckily, Paul Allen knew someone who was working on an operating system, Tim Paterson with Seattle Computer Products, a small microcomputer hardware company based in Washington.[6] Over the course of four months, Paterson developed his QDOS (quick and dirty operating system), later known as 86-DOS.

Microsoft ended up purchasing the future licensing rights to 86-DOS from Seattle Computer Products for $50,000. Gates had called Sams asking about the licensing for the project. "Do you want to get [QDOS], or do you want me to?" Gates asked Sams, according to the former IBM exec. "By all means, you get it," Sams responded.[7]

Those six words ended up netting Microsoft billions of dollars. The operating system—known as PC-DOS, and later MS-DOS—took Microsoft to a new level of prestige and success.

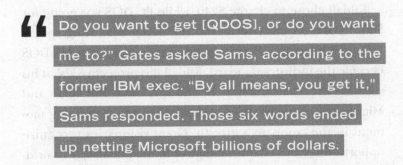

Do you want to get [QDOS], or do you want me to?" Gates asked Sams, according to the former IBM exec. "By all means, you get it," Sams responded. Those six words ended up netting Microsoft billions of dollars.

Instead of getting per-copy royalties from IBM, Microsoft reached a nonexclusive agreement that allowed it to license MS-DOS to other companies. That outside licensing deal was the "real bonanza," Allen recalled[8]—"the product that could be sold over and over again worldwide, under our own name, to companies that would follow IBM's flying wedge to the 16-bit market."

The IBM Personal Computer, model 5150, was a massive success, with three million units sold. A PC for the business world.

Kildall's Folly

If only Gary Kildall had said yes to IBM's demands, Microsoft would have missed its prime opportunity, and Kildall may have soaked up the riches, celebrity, and influence that Bill Gates would eventually have.

IBM came calling, but Kildall wasn't satisfied with the flat fee for the operating system and struggled to recognize the long-term potential the deal would bring.[9] Microsoft capitalized. Kildall saw PC-DOS as a rip-off of CP/M. He considered suing Microsoft and IBM, but he instead ended up reaching his own deal with IBM[10]—a chance to sell CP/M-86, later dubbed DR-DOS.

Kildall chose to charge $240, while PC-DOS was going for $40.[11] DR-DOS was considered the better operating system but not $200 better. Due to its price and availability, MS-DOS became the industry standard. Kildall was protective about his software at a crucial moment, and it allowed Bill Gates and Microsoft to become *Bill Gates* and *Microsoft*—a defining moment in the company's growth. Great visionaries recognize opportunities and take advantage of them. Kildall was a world-class programming mind, but Gates also possessed shrewd business sense.

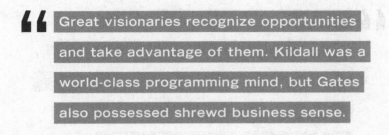

Great visionaries recognize opportunities and take advantage of them. Kildall was a world-class programming mind, but Gates also possessed shrewd business sense.

Ahead of Its Time

Between the IBM partnership and other licensing deals, MS-DOS rose to the top of the PC world. But the company was lacking its own "killer apps" as Apple had with VisiCalc. Charles Simonyi, a lead programmer at Xerox PARC, was hired to lead the company's applications groups. Xerox was using a GUI, or graphical user interface, for its Alto computer, which was revolutionary but wasn't priced for mass consumption.

Xerox was especially ahead of its time in terms of word processing—on the Alto, you could "cut" and "paste" text, and change the style of the font.[12] Prompts were carried out not with a keyboard, but with a mouse you could move with your hand. Using the mouse, you could drag and drop icons in order to perform tasks like printing—a GUI interface that was easy to use.

Slices of the Pie

With Microsoft continuing to grow, leadership chose to incorporate in June 1981. The incorporation meant Microsoft's top employees would get a cut of the company—a step toward an eventual public offering.

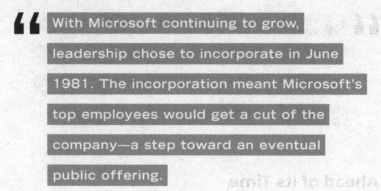

> With Microsoft continuing to grow, leadership chose to incorporate in June 1981. The incorporation meant Microsoft's top employees would get a cut of the company—a step toward an eventual public offering.

Bill Gates: 51 percent.
Paul Allen: 30 percent.
Steve Ballmer: 7.8 percent.

Others receiving stakes included venture capitalist David Marquardt's investment group—a member of Microsoft's board of directors—along with Vern Raburn, Gordon Letwin, and Charles Simonyi.

By the fall of 1981, Microsoft was on the move again, to a larger space near Lake Washington. "Bill and I took adjacent offices with a shared secretary and a short passageway between us," Allen wrote.[13] "I could hear his every shouting match, including the battles royal with Steve Ballmer." As Allen focused more and more on the programming, he got pushed further aside. He wrote Gates a letter in June 1982 stating that he could "no longer tolerate the brow-beating or 'tirades'" and that the "camaraderie of the early days is long since gone." Soon after, Gates hired Jim Towne as Microsoft's president and COO, and he got Allen's office (Towne wouldn't last long).

Big Changes

By 1982, Bill Gates was ready to build on the international success Microsoft had experienced in Japan. "With Kay Nishi's aggressive salesmanship, [Microsoft] bagged the lion's share of the language market there. The reward was millions of dollars in revenue for Microsoft's coffers, almost as much as that pouring into the company from all its US sales," James Wallace and Jim Erickson wrote in the 1992 book *Hard Drive*.[14]

Gates wanted to launch an International Division, and he selected Scott Oki to run it. Oki suggested a series of local agents serving as subsidiaries. It took some time, but as IBM's PC and similar machines running MS-DOS became popular overseas, Microsoft's international success would surpass its domestic sales.[15]

The global focus turned Microsoft's founders into jet-setting salesmen. During a trip to Europe with Gates for a press tour in September 1982, Allen began to feel "as if I had the flu, except there was no fever."[16] He started experiencing a painful itch behind his knees. Night sweats and a bump on the side of his neck followed.

Something wasn't right. Allen flew home. He soon received the diagnosis: Hodgkin's disease. Cancer.

Allen's cancer was treatable. He received radiation treatments and hoped for the best. He was thirty years old, the co-founder of one of the country's fastest-growing companies. Paul Allen had a lot of life ahead of him, a life full of new ventures and opportunities. For him, life was too short to spend it getting cut down by Gates's criticism and ultra-competitiveness. Microsoft had grown stressful and bitter for him. He wasn't defined by the company the way Gates was. He had already begun considering his departure from Microsoft, but the diagnosis made the decision easier for him. Gates and Ballmer were taking Microsoft in a new direction separate from Allen, and on February 18, 1983, Allen resigned from the company he had cofounded. He retained his stock, giving him equity in case the company ever went public. He also remained on Microsoft's board.

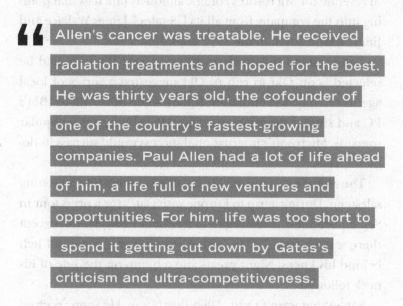

Allen's cancer was treatable. He received radiation treatments and hoped for the best. He was thirty years old, the cofounder of one of the country's fastest-growing companies. Paul Allen had a lot of life ahead of him, a life full of new ventures and opportunities. For him, life was too short to spend it getting cut down by Gates's criticism and ultra-competitiveness.

As Allen faded into the company's past, Gates became its central focus—the north star guiding the company forward.

Growing Pains

Not all of Microsoft's products were massive successes. The company released a spreadsheet program, Multiplan, in 1982, to rival VisiCalc and the popular Lotus 1-2-3. Despite VisiCalc's early impact, Lotus 1-2-3 became the key spreadsheet program of the 1980s and IBM's "killer application," driving success of the IBM PC.

Lotus Development Corporation, which was founded by Mitchell Kapor, released Lotus 1-2-3 in January 1983 for newer versions of the IBM PC—outperforming Multiplan, which had been designed to work on the lower-memory first-generation IBM PCs. Training seminars and clubs devoted to Lotus 1-2-3 cropped up across the country. While selling steadily, Multiplan faded into obscurity. "Multiplan, although [it] contributed a lot of good ideas . . . was essentially passed by with the work that Lotus did on 1-2-3," Gates said.[17]

Word to the Wise

Microsoft's first word processing program was initially going to be called "Multi-Tool Word," until it was rebranded with a shortened, more compelling name: "Microsoft Word."

Microsoft Word was released on October 25, 1983. It was clunky and entered a crowded market featuring more than three hundred different titles including MicroPro, WordPerfect, and MultiMate. But the initial Word also featured lots of elements that still exist in current word processing programs, such as line breaks and bold-faced and italic fonts on-screen—it was the first product of its kind guided by the philosophy "WYSIWYG" ("What You See Is What You Get"), meaning the look of the project on the screen matched the look of the printed page.[18]

Sharp targeted marketing and key updates helped Microsoft Word find its footing, and a free demo disk was included with copies of *PC World* magazine. Microsoft sold Word in tandem with a new product—a slightly curved mouse featuring two green buttons that was manufactured by a Japanese company, Alps. "We tied it to Word so that we had a bundle with Word and the Mouse. But then people who didn't like the Mouse thought they shouldn't buy Word. So, it was a little bit of a problem," Gates said.[19] "When we first brought this out we ordered 50,000 and it took over a year to sell the first 50,000."

Not-So-Bitter Apple

Long before they became rivals, Apple and Microsoft were friendly. Apple's showman of a cofounder, Steve Jobs, invited Gates to his company's Cupertino offices in the early 1980s to present some projects he'd been developing, and by 1982 a contract was signed. Microsoft ended up developing a slate of programs—Multiplan, Chart, Word, File, and BASIC—for Apple's Macintosh, later branded the 128K, which was released in early 1984 after long delays. In the inaugural issue of *Macworld*, Microsoft's advertisement appears on the inside cover. "Microsoft's greatest hits are now playing on Macintosh," the headline claims.

The issue also featured an interview with Gates.[20] "I think the Mac will mean that there's at least one company besides IBM in the personal computer business that doesn't have to do everything the IBM way," he said.

Jobs also invited Gates to an Apple sales conference to participate in a presentation called "Macintosh Software Dating Game" alongside Fred Gibbons with Software Publishing Co., and Mitch Kapor of Lotus Development.[21]

"Software magnate No. 3, when was your first date with Macintosh?" Jobs asked.

"We've been working with the Mac for almost two years now, and we put some of our really good people on it," Gates responded.

At another point during the presentation, Jobs inquired about Macintosh's quality.

"To create a new standard, it takes something that's not just a little bit different, it takes something that's really new and really captures people's imagination. And the Macintosh, of all the machines I've ever seen, is the only one that meets that standard."

At the end of the skit, it was time for Jobs to pick his ideal date. "Apples are red, IBM's blue, if Mac's going to be the third milestone, I need all of you," he told the execs.

But by the time of the Macintosh launch, the Jobs-Gates relationship was starting to sour. A few months earlier, Gates had announced that Microsoft would be developing a GUI for IBM PCs called Windows. Jobs saw Windows as a blatant rip-off of Apple's interface. Their contract stipulated that Microsoft wouldn't create graphical software for other companies until a year after the Macintosh was released (it was initially scheduled to be shipped in January 1983). But was it Gates's fault that the Macintosh was delayed a year? And Windows would be released in 1985, far more than a year later than the contract stipulated.

Jobs had Gates travel to Cupertino. He was going to let him have it.

Gates, as he recalled years later,[22] faced down Jobs and nearly a dozen other Apple employees. Jobs accused Gates of stealing from the company. "Well, Steve, I think there's more than one way of looking at it. I think it's more like we both had this rich neighbor named Xerox and I broke into his house to steal the TV set and found out that you had already stolen it," Gates said.

Microsoft's "Killer Apps"

Microsoft's "killer apps" were released and refined, one after another. Version 2.0 of Microsoft Word—released in February 1985—included a spell-checker and word counter. A few months later, moving on from Multiplan, Microsoft announced its next spreadsheet program, dubbed Microsoft Excel.[23] Excel was initially developed for the Apple's Macintosh 512K.

Microsoft's long-term strategy, at least during the mid-1980s, still included a strong partnership with IBM. The companies reached a joint development agreement involving operating systems and other software products—and OS/2 was underway.

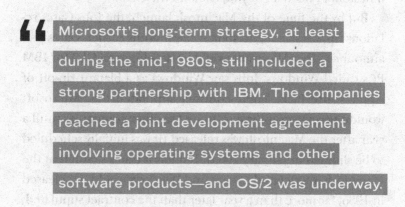

> Microsoft's long-term strategy, at least during the mid-1980s, still included a strong partnership with IBM. The companies reached a joint development agreement involving operating systems and other software products—and OS/2 was underway.

The agreement put the companies on a more level playing field, and allowed Microsoft to sell operating systems to other manufacturers. It also put Microsoft and IBM on a crash course—Microsoft's long-gestating GUI to run MS-DOS, called Windows, was finally released in November 1985 after years of delays, in direct competition of IBM's TopView program.

The roots of Microsoft Windows date back to 1981, when development began on a project then called Interface Manager.[24] The goal: "Interface Manager finally fulfills the promise of ease-of-use, software portability and an open applications environment with specs readily available/affordable so software is available and standardized across many computers." Interface Manager was going to make software easier to use.

The initial Windows offering flopped, an incomplete operating system featuring tiled windows—overlapping windows aren't allowed in the first version of Windows—and features such as a calculator, clipboard viewer, clock, notepad, paint, and the word processor Write.

Between Windows, Word, Excel, and MS-DOS, Microsoft was fulfilling its vision of "a computer on every desk, and in every home, running Microsoft software." The programs weren't all top performers in their class—Microsoft Windows still had a long way to go—but the programs were readily available, ran on numerous computers, and were affordably priced or bundled, ready for a mass audience, to be used with the latest hardware.

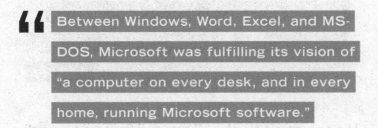

> Between Windows, Word, Excel, and MS-DOS, Microsoft was fulfilling its vision of "a computer on every desk, and in every home, running Microsoft software."

Microsoft was a ubiquitous presence. And its business model showed sky-high potential, motivating Gates to methodically take the steps to make Microsoft a publicly traded company.

According to *Fortune*: "Unlike its competitors, Microsoft was not dominated by venture capital investors hungry to harvest some of their gains. The business gushed cash. With pretax profits running as high as 34 percent of revenues, Microsoft needed no outside money to expand. Most important, Gates values control of his time and his company more than personal wealth."[25]

Critics wondered about Microsoft's long-term outlook, especially given that other companies such as Lotus had struggled after going public. But Lotus only had a $13 million revenue in the year before its IPO in 1983—less than one-tenth of Microsoft's 1985 revenue. Microsoft's market valuation was much higher, too. And it had Bill Gates.

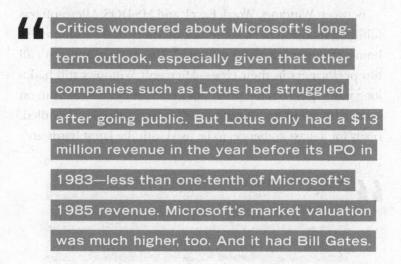

> Critics wondered about Microsoft's long-term outlook, especially given that other companies such as Lotus had struggled after going public. But Lotus only had a $13 million revenue in the year before its IPO in 1983—less than one-tenth of Microsoft's 1985 revenue. Microsoft's market valuation was much higher, too. And it had Bill Gates.

"The company is clearly well-run, well-financed, and well-respected," John Gantz wrote in the March 17, 1986, issue of *InfoWorld.* Gantz speculated that Microsoft was "just at the crest of its glory" due to diminishing demand for MS-DOS, IBM's eventual divorce from Microsoft, and Microsoft's long-term focus on application software, "a tough and fragmented market."[26]

Gates was worried what impact Wall Street success could have on his company. Would it result in a mass exodus of now-rich employees—that with untold riches would come a wave of thirty-year-old retirees and mass departures? Or would it be tougher to lure execs in the future without the opportunity to offer stakes in the company, as Microsoft had with Charles Simonyi?

"With the market sort of maybe over-anticipating the future, or getting paranoid—you know the stock would be very volatile. But I was convinced that it made sense. And as long as we were going to do it, it was an opportunity to really expose the company broadly," Gates said.[27]

CFO Frank Gaudette selected underwriters, and as the IPO process evolved, Gates constantly grappled over the price, trying to keep it modest to avoid an early slide. Microsoft went public on March 13, 1986, and was first traded at $25.50 a share after being priced at $21. Gates's 45 percent stake in the company meant he was soon worth billions as he entered his thirties.

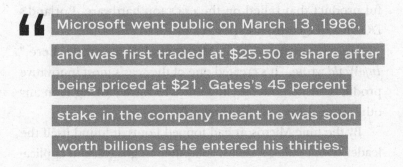

Microsoft went public on March 13, 1986, and was first traded at $25.50 a share after being priced at $21. Gates's 45 percent stake in the company meant he was soon worth billions as he entered his thirties.

Reaching the Top

Microsoft unseated Lotus in 1987 as the top seller of PC software. By the mid-1980s, Lotus 1-2-3 carried more than 80 percent of the spreadsheet market share for PCs—the "killer app" for IBM computers. It was foolish for Microsoft to challenge Lotus on its own turf. Instead, Microsoft looked for opportunities and forced Lotus into a position of weakness.

Firstly, Microsoft reached an exclusive contract to develop its Multiplan spreadsheet for Mac, neutralizing Lotus from releasing its most popular program. But Apple was still interested in working with Lotus, and ended up reaching a deal for a suite of applications, Jazz. And Jazz was a mess—full of glitches and bugs, and at $595, too pricey to make the right impact.

"We spent a fortune on advertising, including TV advertising, which was one of the worst business decisions I ever made. It was just like setting fire to bales of hundred-dollar bills," Kapor told CNet in 2014.[28]

As Lotus spent time, money, and effort trying to improve Jazz—energy it wasn't devoting to 1-2-3 for PC—Microsoft was improving Excel with a graphics-based approach and more perks to its Windows-based spreadsheet, and building a powerful product that relied on the era's top hardware. Borland's DOS-based Quattro also posed a threat to Lotus.

"We're convinced that Microsoft has a winner here," *InfoWorld* wrote. "It's created one of the year's most innovative products, more powerful and more forward-looking than any other spreadsheet on the market."[29]

By the time Microsoft had topped Lotus, it found itself the leader in operating systems, computer languages, and applications software—as well as the leading developer of Mac business software. "Now Microsoft is preparing to unveil new programs in the only major product area where it has failed to produce a major hit: the market for IBM-compatible business applications such as financial analysis, database management and word processing," the *Los Angeles Times* wrote.[30]

Microsoft also released Microsoft Bookshelf, a compact disc featuring reference e-books such as Roget's Thesaurus, in 1987. The circular CDs were the disk of the future, able to hold roughly 680 megabytes of digital information; a typical floppy disk holds 1.44 MB.

Good Forethought

Through its first decade, Microsoft didn't deal much in acquisitions; it instead favored partnerships and licensing deals. But Forethought, a company based in Sunnyvale, California, made a program that allowed Apple Macintosh users to create presentations: PowerPoint.

Microsoft was interested in adding PowerPoint to its stable of business products. So it purchased Forethought in July 1987 for $14 million—the largest acquisition in the company's history up to that point.

Big Blue's Big Battle

IBM was ready to fight the clones. "Big Blue" had seen its market share erode during the 1980s—a reflection of IBM's decisions to use off-the-shelf technology and license an operating system, MS-DOS, that was also licensed to other manufacturers. IBM's PC was revolutionary, but as the years passed, it was no longer unique. The Personal Computer AT, released in 1984, involved architecture that was mostly open—leading to further cloning.

IBM prepared its third generation of personal computers, the Personal System/2, or PS/2, for release in 1987. IBM wanted to create an industry standard—with machines that were 80 percent made by IBM. The lowest price of the three PS/2 models came with a price tag of $1,695.

Microsoft's second IBM operating system, OS/2, was announced on April 2, 1987, and released that December for the PS/2, to general indifference. It didn't pair with any "killer applications." In fact, applications needed to be upgraded to run on OS/2, and memory and disk storage came into play. Industry experts predicted OS/2 would become the industry standard by 1990. But the partnership and OS/2 languished amid the strain of the two companies' cultures, said Nathan Myhrvold, who guided Microsoft's research efforts during the 1990s and served as chief technology officer. Myhrvold, outspoken and bright, worked under famed theoretical physicist Stephen Hawking while holding a postdoctoral fellowship. He bonded with Gates after joining Microsoft in 1986 when his company was purchased by Microsoft.

Early on in his Microsoft tenure, Myhrvold was tasked with working on the OS/2 project, and he says he quickly recognized it was doomed. "IBM had an agenda that was set by the fact that they were a mainframe software company and they kept trying to find some reason that that would be important in the PC world," Myhrvold said. IBM wanted to create common system application architecture between its giant mainframes and PCs, which only made sense to IBM. The code was larger and slower, and IBM was plagued by corporate groupthink. "We were genuinely afraid that they would make OS/2 into something that was so pathetic that no PC industry applications would be developed for it and the whole thing would fail," Myhrvold said. Microsoft pleaded with its partner to keep Windows competitive. But after IBM's Presentation Manager bombed, IBM employees suggested Microsoft hobble Windows, Myhrvold said.

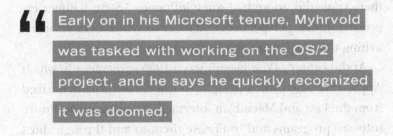

" Early on in his Microsoft tenure, Myhrvold was tasked with working on the OS/2 project, and he says he quickly recognized it was doomed.

But that wasn't going to happen.

Tech Tussle

Shared innovation was a way of life in the software world of the 1980s. Once one company developed a technology, other companies rushed to create their own version, a never-ending arms race. Apple prided itself as being different, exclusive, prestigious—those characteristics, along with its graphic user interface, helped separate the Macintosh from the pack.

But by the late 1980s, PC developments started to share a lot of similarities with Apple innovations. Windows 2.03 featured tiled windows, and icons, and was directed by mouse clicks. Apple's graphical user interface featured tiled windows, and icons, and was directed by mouse clicks. So Apple decided to protect its interest by suing Microsoft, as well as Hewlett-Packard, for its upcoming New Wave software in March 1988 in San Francisco federal district court, alleging that the companies stole the "look and feel" of the Macintosh.

Gates fought back. "We're saying that these graphic interface techniques, the ideas, are not copyrightable," he told *InfoWorld* following the lawsuit. Additionally, Gates argued, "[Microsoft] had more people working on Macintosh software than Apple did, so we had some influence." Steve Ballmer expressed similar perspectives in a letter to Windows developers, writing that the lawsuit was "without merit."[31]

At the center of the lawsuit was a 1985 agreement in which Apple gave Microsoft the right to use visual displays derived from the Lisa and Macintosh interfaces "in present and future software programs and to license them to and through third parties for use in their software programs." In exchange, Microsoft gave Apple the opportunity to license any new visual displays created by Microsoft for a period of five years.

If anyone deserved credit for the innovations, it was Xerox, which had developed the first GUI, an innovation that fueled and inspired successful releases by Apple and Microsoft. But the lawsuit was a scary prospect for Microsoft, and fueled anxiety about upcoming releases—opening the possibility that Windows could be derailed or users would avoid it. Microsoft remained committed to moving ahead with its projects, regardless of the looming court battle.

Gates and Microsoft had been resolute a decade earlier when facing arbitration against MITS and Pertec. Apple was merely the next threat. Apple's lawsuit—while in many measures overreaching—hinted at factors that would lead to Microsoft's darkest days.

But Microsoft wasn't worried about getting *too big* as the 1980s came to a close. Bill Gates's company had grown in every measure—it went from two dozen employees in 1980 to about six thousand local employees a decade later. Microsoft went from developing the first microcomputer language to dominating the software market, a ubiquitous presence that was well on its way of accomplishing Gates's goal of a computer on every desk, and in every home, running Microsoft software.

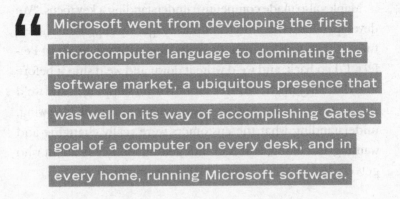

> **Microsoft went from developing the first microcomputer language to dominating the software market, a ubiquitous presence that was well on its way of accomplishing Gates's goal of a computer on every desk, and in every home, running Microsoft software.**

An "Adult" Joins the Mix

As Microsoft entered adolescence, it needed a seasoned hand to guide its applications.

Longtime IBM exec Mike Maples joined Microsoft in 1988. At forty-six, Maples was more than a decade older than most of the company's employees and enjoyed dressing in suits and ties. He affectionately called himself Microsoft's "designated adult."[32]

And the "designated adult" made quick changes, splitting the applications software division into five business units: the office business unit (overseeing Microsoft Word and Microsoft Mail), graphics business unit (PowerPoint), entry business unit (Works, Learning DOS, and Flight Simulator), data access business unit (File and Quick Basic), and analysis business unit (Excel, Multiplan, and Project).[33] The reorganization meant each division was effectively treated as its own start-up—and allowed Microsoft to foster a "small company attitude" despite its expanding revenue.[34] Focusing each application on its core, central strengths brought out the value in each—and bundling the apps together gave consumers added value, a chance to have many needs met from one purchase.

Maples also made competitive understanding a key focus. "We developed tools that would allow us to quickly implement [a feature]. I'd go to a business show and see a feature in Word Perfect, I'd go back, and we'd write it down and we'd ship it before they did. They might be three months from shipping it, and we'd ship in two months. And so it was a matter of quick following, understanding what the customers were really changing and wanting and liking, and then not getting too heady about who gets credit," Maples said in a 2018 podcast interview.[35]

"The Most Brilliant Person"

Mario Juarez remembers his first real face time with Gates. The Microsoft communications staffer presented Gates with a fifteen-page background briefing document ahead of an uplink interview with a TV network. Gates's technical assistant gave Juarez a piece of advice: while Gates reads the document, you need to talk to him and pitch your narrative. "Bill processes both tracks simultaneously," the assistant said. Juarez watched as Gates scanned the document, rocking forward and backward.

"He's looking through the pages so fast, I'm like, 'He can't be reading it.' And then I get done talking," Juarez said. And sure enough, Gates highlighted the one weak point of the document.[36]

Gates went and gave the interview, reciting the talking points nearly verbatim. "He didn't only have an engineering mind, he had a great business mind, and he knew how to read a situation and find a weakness and go in and exploit it and see the opportunity," said Juarez, who would work consistently with Gates.

"He was just overwhelmingly brilliant and he was the most brilliant person in a company full of brilliant people." In terms of the company's success: "In some ways it was the stars just perfectly aligning. But let's be really, really clear about the bright star in the middle, which was Bill Gates," Juarez said.

Juarez saw similarities between Gates's oversight of Microsoft and Chicago Bulls star Michael Jordan's success on the basketball court. "When Michael Jordan was in his prime, you would just watch him move, and you could see that he was just naturally gifted beyond everybody else on the court. He could fly. He would jump, and it was like, 'How can anyone jump that high and fly that far and then with that much precision?' Jordan's other factor was that he wanted it more than anyone else, that he worked harder than anyone else. And that was Bill Gates. Bill had this work ethic that was just absolutely obsessive, and it sort of permeated the company that you were going to work."[37]

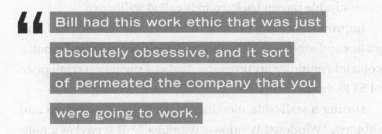

Bill had this work ethic that was just absolutely obsessive, and it sort of permeated the company that you were going to work.

Gates was right most of the time, or he could wear someone down until they conceded. But that wasn't always the case, former Chief Technology Officer Nathan Myhrvold says. "Bill is super smart and he's super focused and he would take strong views on things, but if he was wrong, he was also happy to hear he was wrong. And I think that is what endeared him to me. You totally could tell him he was wrong, and he'd think about it, and he'd say, 'Oh, OK. You're right.' And of course a lot of people, particularly if they're a big grand pooh-bah kind of a situation, they're a CEO, they're not willing to say they're wrong," Myhrvold said. "He was also tolerant of when I was wrong because nobody's always right. He was interested in what the best approach was."

Windows! Windows! Windows!

Windows 3.0 arrived on May 22, 1990. The graphical user interface was developed for a standard one-megabyte personal computer, meaning about 60 percent of MS-DOS users could install and use it. It also featured a user shell that allowed for managing applications and files without leaving Windows. Users could open Windows without worrying about inputting MS-DOS commands. It featured colorful icons that could be rearranged and customizable screen backgrounds called wallpaper.

Improved memory made it run faster, and it came with fun games and accessories like the card game Solitaire and Paint, a colorful computer art program. And at a suggested retail price of $149, it was affordable.

During a staff-wide meeting, Steve Ballmer stood up and shouted, "Windows! Windows! Windows!"[38] It served as a rallying cry for the rank-and-file employees. Microsoft was finally moving out of IBM's shadow.

The strategy seemed like a suicide mission for many staffers. IBM, in large part, had put Microsoft on the map with the PC-DOS partnership. And then there was the bait-and-switch feel of *Windows! Windows! Windows!* Microsoft spent years selling PC users—and software development companies—on OS/2 and Presentation Manager. Now, Microsoft would be shifting focus away from OS/2 and IBM to promote its own competing product, and software developers would need to choose Windows or OS/2.

Windows 3 ended up selling four million copies in its first year—establishing Microsoft's dominance in the new decade. That dominance caused the decade-long dalliance between IBM and Microsoft to fall apart—Windows 3.0 was being bundled with new computers, while OS/2 was being pushed aside. The victor became clearer in October 1990 when Microsoft released Office for Windows, bundling three of its applications for Windows 3.0: Word, Excel, and PowerPoint—one of the masterstrokes of Mike Maples's guidance of the apps division. Other companies were only releasing individual copies of word processors, spreadsheet and presentation tools, and Microsoft could offer discounts for the suite over purchases for individual applications. Uniformity across the individual applications also drove adaptation.

"The genius of the idea of combining them . . . changed everything and it quickly emerged as the right thing," Juarez said. "It's as impossible to imagine Microsoft today without Office as it is without Windows."[39]

Versions of Windows 3.1—released between 1992 and 1993—brought on the "Multimedia PC" with its use of CD-ROM drives and sound cards.[40] Windows 3.1 featured improved system stability, TrueType fonts, and the ability to drag and drop programs, and it sold more than three million copies within its first few months of release.

"It was actually Windows 3.1 where the rocket ship lifted off the pad," recalls Juarez. "You couldn't print copies fast enough."[41]

Nathan Myhrvold compared the Microsoft-IBM split to a divorced couple "where, as soon as the divorce occurs, both of the people totally reform." Suddenly, IBM was doing all the things Microsoft had asked years earlier. "If they had done that stuff and listened to us in the first place, we never would have broken up. And OS/2 would have been the standard thing and IBM would have owned a big piece of it. As it stands, the way the deal had been done, IBM didn't own Windows, Microsoft did. And because Windows wasn't hobbled with all of this shit that no one wanted, it was better," Myrhvold said.

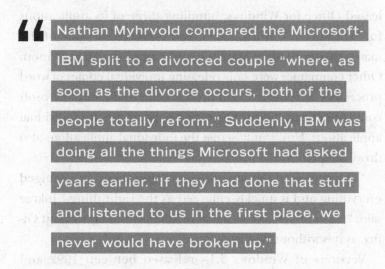

> Nathan Myhrvold compared the Microsoft-IBM split to a divorced couple "where, as soon as the divorce occurs, both of the people totally reform." Suddenly, IBM was doing all the things Microsoft had asked years earlier. "If they had done that stuff and listened to us in the first place, we never would have broken up."

Research and Development

Myhrvold was an inquisitive type, one to come up with ideas about all different sorts of things. He approached Bill Gates in 1990 with an idea. Why not create a research division? Up to that point, the PC world had focused mainly on taking developments on mainframe computers and reproducing them for PCs. Getting cheaper and faster, PCs were going to get super-fast in the coming years. Additionally, Microsoft shouldn't have to rely on other outlets like Xerox PARC to innovate.

People inside Microsoft thought Myhrvold was crazy, he says. "It was very controversial at Microsoft with everyone other than

Bill," Myhrvold said. But with Gates's approval, Microsoft Research was a reality, and it would end up driving innovation across the company and tech world.

That "M" Word

Not only was Microsoft becoming the dominant company for computer language and applications, now it also had the graphic user interface that ran those applications. Industry experts began tossing around the word "monopoly."

"With Microsoft on top, most of Bill's remaining friends are his shareholders. Bill's speeches, long a source of vision for the open PC industry, have become self-serving outlines of Microsoft's rapacious product plans. Bill's industry partnerships have turned one-sided and sour. And Bill's company, known in the past for drawing new customers to a burgeoning industry, is spending too much of its considerable energy on damaging dependent competitors in a stagnant market," Bob Metcalfe, who invented Ethernet and founded 3Com Corp, wrote in a 1991 *Computerworld* column.[42] "If Microsoft's abuse of its monopoly isn't illegal, it ought to be."

One major gripe for computer industry insiders such as Metcalfe: Microsoft would take ideas developed by other companies, then introduce or adapt those updates to an upcoming Windows release or roll out its own competing application. Such was the case with Go Corp., which announced a pen-based operating system, PenPoint OS, in 1991, only to see Microsoft discussing pen-based extensions for Windows.

Gates could argue that everything was a free-for-all, and everyone was copying off of each other—a main point of Microsoft's argument against Apple's lawsuit—but his company was far removed from the days of his "Open Letter to the Hobby" decrying companies stealing from each other. Microsoft's MO after its first fifteen years in existence: Microsoft knew better. Innovation went through Microsoft.

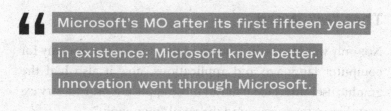

> **Microsoft's MO after its first fifteen years in existence: Microsoft knew better. Innovation went through Microsoft.**

An Investigation Begins

Microsoft developed an industry standard that was adopted by other software providers, then decided to go in a completely different direction with Windows 3.0, known as its "deep head-fake." The shift left other developers scrambling—Microsoft was constantly moving the goalposts.

As Microsoft gained traction with its programs on its operating systems, competitors like Lotus were at a disadvantage, and their market shares evaporated.

The government doesn't happen to like it when companies exert so much control over the market, and the Federal Trade Commission, an independent government agency focused on consumer protection, initiated an investigation into Microsoft's monopolistic practices.[43] The investigation—which initially focused on the agreement between IBM and Microsoft—expanded to include a number of allegations, including:

▪ That Microsoft gave its developers of applications software information about its operating systems software before providing it to other applications developers;

- That Microsoft announced that it was developing a nonexistent version of operating software—"vaporware"—to dissuade Original Equipment Manufacturers from leasing a competitor's operating system;
- That Microsoft required OEMs that licensed its operating system software also to license Microsoft applications; and
- That Microsoft licensed its operating systems to OEMs on a per-processor basis.

Gates and Microsoft remained resilient in the face of government scrutiny, even as Microsoft's stock price tumbled. Never surrender. As far as Gates and his company were concerned, people were simply jealous of Microsoft's success.

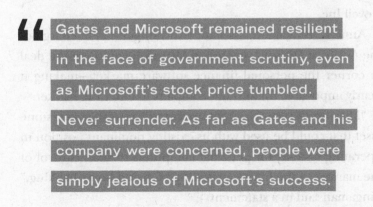

Gates and Microsoft remained resilient in the face of government scrutiny, even as Microsoft's stock price tumbled. Never surrender. As far as Gates and his company were concerned, people were simply jealous of Microsoft's success.

This was the price you paid when you became the biggest software company in the world, with yearly revenues topping $1 billion. Microsoft wasn't a scrappy upstart anymore.

The FTC couldn't reach a decision on Microsoft—its commissioners deadlocked 2–2 in a 1993 vote. So, the Antitrust Division of the Department of Justice decided to take the reins of the investigation, and in 1994 the DOJ and Microsoft reached a settlement agreement. As part of the settlement, Microsoft signed a consent decree barring it from using its operating systems to crush competitors. The consent decree included the mention of an upcoming product code-named "Chicago."

Everything was gravy until April 1995, when Microsoft announced a $2 billion deal to buy Intuit Inc., the maker of personal finance software such as Quicken. Quicken had a 70 percent market share and more than seven million users. Microsoft's Money was the second-ranked personal finance title, with about 22 percent market share.

Within days, the DOJ's Antitrust Division filed a lawsuit to block the merger, suggesting the deal "would likely lead to higher prices and lessened innovation in the market." The DOJ also balked at Microsoft's plan to shift its Money assets to Novell Inc.

Anne K. Bingaman, assistant attorney general in charge of the Antitrust Division, suggested Microsoft could use the deal to corner the personal finance software market—making it nearly impossible for another company to enter the market.

"Microsoft's control of that market will give it a cornerstone asset that could be used with its existing dominant position in operating systems for personal computers to seize control of the markets of the future, including PC-based home banking," Bingaman said in a statement.

The deal was dead. But the government's attempts to rein in Microsoft were only going to intensify.

Melinda

Melinda French stood out. A Microsoft hire with a master's from Duke University, she was the only woman among her recruiting class of MBAs when she was hired in 1987. She served as a product manager for projects like Word and Money and Encarta and the much-derided Microsoft Bob, and earned the title of general manager of information products.

Melinda was brilliant and bubbly and charming, and she caught Bill Gates's eye. Melinda and Bill dated off and on for about five years before getting engaged in 1993. They were married the following year.

But the time period was bittersweet for Bill—his mother was battling cancer. She died in June 1994. Before the wedding, Mary Gates wrote a letter to Melinda, offering advice about life and marriage. "From those to whom much is given, much is expected," she wrote.[44]

That mentality inspired the young couple—Bill and Melinda endowed a $10 million scholarship at the University of Washington in his mother's name, and they later established the William H. Gates foundation.[45]

Melinda and Bill matched and complemented and completed each other. And as their family grew with three children, and they settled into Xanadu 2.0, the futuristic "earth-sheltered" mansion that took Gates seven years to build, and their fortune continued to accrue, they didn't forget Mary Gates's advice.

"Windows 95 is so easy,
even a talk show host
could figure it out."

—BILL GATES,
Cofounder of Microsoft

CHAPTER THREE

A NEW STRATOSPHERE

I f you start me up . . .

Bill Gates's rock star moment had arrived. Microsoft's campus had turned into a giant festival. Crowds at dozens of global locations, seven hundred thousand people in all, simultaneously watched on, cheering as *Tonight Show* host Jay Leno invited Gates to the stage. The Rolling Stones' famous hit played in the background.

If you start me up I'll never stop . . .

The song was a part of the moment—Microsoft had paid anywhere from $1.5 to $10 million to license it, depending on what you believe, to properly celebrate the start of something big, something that started with "Start," a new product called Windows 95.[1]

During the launch event, Leno, a neophyte who didn't use a computer until about a month before the launch party, riffed on current events, tech culture, and Gates's wealth. Addressing the crowd as "Microsofties," he highlighted the meaning behind his network's call letters: "Now Bill Compatible."

"This is a man so successful, his chauffeur is Ross Perot," Leno said of Gates, name-dropping the computer pioneer and presidential candidate who once tried, unsuccessfully, to buy Microsoft.[2]

After Leno introduced Gates to the stage, the pair settled into a routine, the tech-averse talk show host and brainiac computer wiz. "I'm kind of a computer virgin here, Bill, and as we go through this, I hope you'll be gentle, I hope you'll be kind," Leno said.

"Windows 95 is so easy, even a talk show host could figure it out," Gates responded to hoots and hollers.

Gates, standing proud in his navy polo and khakis, exuded cool—maybe not Rolling Stones cool, or even Jay Leno cool, but he was a man in his moment. Twenty years into Microsoft's life span, and twelve years after Windows was first conceived, Gates was on top of the world and his product was a smash success.

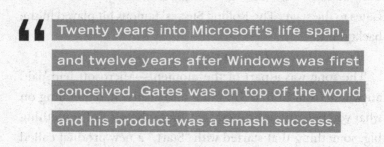

> Twenty years into Microsoft's life span, and twelve years after Windows was first conceived, Gates was on top of the world and his product was a smash success.

Marketing Windows 95

Microsoft made sure Windows 95 was everywhere. TV commercials featuring the Rolling Stones' "Start Me Up" aired nationwide,[3] and Microsoft paid to light the façade of New York City's Empire State Building in the company's colors—yellow, red, and green.

Maybe the most curious pop culture crossover involved a thirty-minute video guide for Windows 95 featuring *Friends* sitcom stars Jennifer Aniston and Matthew Perry visiting the Microsoft office. "Task bars, and email, and shortcuts, oh my," they said, highlighting the program's features as they walk through the hallway.[4] They eventually reach Gates's office, where they are met by his assistant, Bernice Keppleman (played by Marilyn Pasekoff). After some playful banter, Aniston sits at Gates's desk and clicks the Windows 95 "start" button. "Look, Matty, I'm computing," she says. The pair learn about all of Windows 95's features with the help of an assorted mix of visitors: a window washer, a sleazy computer enthusiast named Chipster (don't ask), a food delivery worker, a boy called "Joystick Johnny," and a grunge band.

Chipster, while extolling the program's potential, also tries to win Aniston's interest (she is not interested). "Where do you want to go today? Think of Windows 95—and me—as the vehicle to get you there. . . . Communicating online is the hot thing right now, and the Microsoft network is your on-ramp to the information superhighway."

People who bought the Windows 95 CD-ROM found another surprise—a file featuring the music video for Weezer's hit song "Buddy Holly" that shows the band, through crafty videography and editing, performing at Arnold's Drive-In on the 1970s sitcom *Happy Days*. Weezer wasn't aware that the video would be included, due to negotiations by their label, and when they found out they weren't happy . . . at first.[5] But the video meant massive exposure.

What Made Windows 95 Great

Beyond gimmicks, ads, and launch events, Windows 95 succeeded because it provided what people needed out of their computer—a smart, practical, visual interface that was easy enough for anyone, computer users or non-users, to operate. Windows 95 opened up the possibility of the PC for everyone, an operating system for the masses. New features drove its success, starting with the Start menu and task bar, which allowed you to keep active windows in a central location (usually the bottom of the screen). The "recycle bin" was added to the desktop for the first time, providing a chance to drag and drop files that you wish to remove. "Minimize" and "maximize" features were added in the upper right-hand corner of the screen, and file naming became streamlined. Windows 95 launched or popularized many features that are still in use today—for all that's changed with computers, from mobile technology to cloud storage, a typical computer desktop twenty-five years later is pretty similar to the one on Windows 95.

In its first year, Windows 95 sold forty million copies. Windows 95—along with the rise of the internet—triggered a personal computer boom.[6] By 1995, about a quarter of US households had a computer. By 2000, that number would cross 50 percent.

Windows 95 required many computer users to upgrade their software, and it fueled interest for memory chips, printers, CD-ROM drives, and applications software. It could be seen as a net benefit for the personal computer industry. It could also be seen as Microsoft's latest vehicle to dominate the market.

"The biggest beneficiary by far of the new software will be Microsoft, and the company's firm grip on the PC industry threatens to become a stranglehold. An avalanche of new Microsoft applications—from spreadsheets to word processors to multimedia encyclopedias—will be ready when Windows 95 is released," the *Los Angeles Times* wrote. "Microsoft's competitors in these areas, less familiar with Windows 95, are mostly still struggling to finish their products."[7]

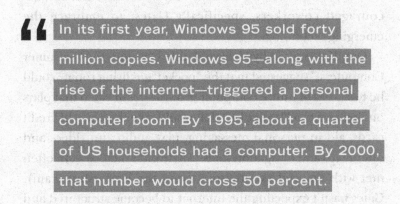

In its first year, Windows 95 sold forty million copies. Windows 95—along with the rise of the internet—triggered a personal computer boom. By 1995, about a quarter of US households had a computer. By 2000, that number would cross 50 percent.

The biggest losers with the release of Windows 95 were IBM and Apple, two fading superpowers who'd partnered with Microsoft, only to see Microsoft bypass them. IBM was still clinging to the OS/2, the operating system it had been developing with Microsoft before Windows became the industry standard. Apple, meanwhile, expressed bitterness and hostility as Windows 95 was poised to eat away its eroding market share. Apple wasn't fresh anymore.

The Missing Piece

Despite all of its hype and celebrity endorsements and popularity and success, Windows 95 was missing something pretty significant when it first launched—a web browser. Microsoft, as it has with numerous forms of emerging technology, struggled to figure out how to properly capitalize on the internet, a World Wide Web that allowed users to connect to a network and visit websites in real time. Internal memos in the early- to mid-1990s by two employees—programmer J Allard, and research czar Nathan Myhrvold—raised the alarm about the internet and encouraged coworkers, specifically Gates, to embrace the emerging technology.[8]

One 1993 memo by Myhrvold, titled "Visions for Consumer Computers," suggested that the "pocket and living room" could be two areas of future computer growth—from video that plays on demand to a "Wallet PC" that would take the place of credit cards, aid in personal messaging, play audio and video, and offer maps and navigation tools (Myrhvold's memos were often met with amused skepticism among the leadership team). Gates wasn't expecting the internet to become structured and organized so quickly. By the time he understood, it was too late to bundle a web browser for Windows 95 1.0, and another company—Netscape Navigator—had already jumped to a commanding lead in market share.

Gates began writing himself, and the message spilled out of him, a long and detailed letter to Microsoft's executive staff and direct reports. He titled the May 26, 1995, memo "The Internet Tidal Wave."[9]

He began: "Our vision for the last 20 years can be summarized in a succinct way. We saw that exponential improvements in computer capabilities would make great software quite valuable. Our response was to build an organization to deliver the best software products. In the next 20 years the improvement in computer power will be outpaced by the exponential improvements in communications networks. The combination of these elements will have a fundamental impact on work, learning and play." Gates was assigning the internet "the highest level of importance. . . . I want to make clear that our focus on the internet is critical to every part of our business."

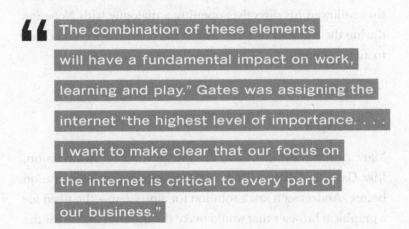

The combination of these elements will have a fundamental impact on work, learning and play." Gates was assigning the internet "the highest level of importance. . . . I want to make clear that our focus on the internet is critical to every part of our business."

He compared the impact of the internet to the IBM PC in 1981, for which Microsoft provided the PC-DOS operating system. "The PC wasn't perfect. Aspects of the PC were arbitrary or even poor. However a phenomena grew up around the IBM PC that made it a key element of everything that would happen for the next 15 years. Companies that tried to fight the PC standard often had good reasons for doing so but they failed because the phenomena overcame any weaknesses that resisters identified." Gates described Netscape as "a new competitor 'born' on the Internet.

"Their browser is dominant, with 70 percent usage share, allowing them to determine which network extensions will catch on. They are pursuing a multi-platform strategy where they move the key API into the client to commoditize the underlying operating system. They have attracted a number of public network operators to use their platform to offer information and directory services. We have to match and beat their offerings including working with MCI, newspapers, and others who are considering their products."

High-ranking Microsoft employees read Gates's memo, and they followed his directive, opening a dialogue with Netscape during the summer of 1995. Maybe the companies could come to an agreement . . .

Netscape

Marc Andreessen was another college student with a vision. Like Gates and Allen with their BASIC interpreter a generation before, Andreessen saw a solution for a problem—the need for a graphical browser that would make the internet usable for the masses. Andreessen, with the help of fellow students at the National Center for Supercomputing Applications at the University of Illinois at Urbana-Champaign, developed the first browser, Mosaic, in 1993. Mosaic was available for free for noncommercial use.

The browser unlocked the internet's visual potential and broke it free from programming language. Where Andreessen saw tech potential, entrepreneur and computer scientist Jim Clark saw commercial opportunity. The duo teamed up to cofound Netscape in April 1994. The company got to work building a new, better browser, and Navigator was born.[10] Netscape Navigator strove to unseat NCSA Mosaic as the leading browser, a goal that Netscape quickly reached. The browser was easy to use and helped users to unlock the internet's potential. Instead of simply scrolling through text-only pages, users could listen to audio and watch video.

When Netscape went public in August 1995—the same month as the Windows 95 launch—Andreessen became a hot commodity, and well on his way to becoming a billionaire, at age twenty-four. He was pictured on the February 19, 1996, cover of *Time* magazine—barefoot, his mouth open, sitting in a chair fit for a king.[11] This was a long way from Bill Gates's 1984 cover showing him balancing a floppy disk on his finger.

Netscape's success motivated companies to develop their own websites, giving them a whole new way to reach potential customers. Where Microsoft was interested in keeping its users in the Windows ecosystem and using Microsoft products, Netscape's browser allowed people to branch out like never before. By Q2 in 1995, Netscape had generated $10 million in revenue by its browser, and that revenue would spike to $45 million by the end of the year. Netscape was on a collision course with the giant. It had awakened Microsoft.[12]

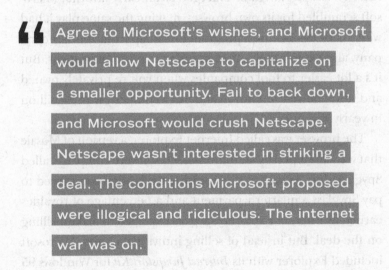

" Agree to Microsoft's wishes, and Microsoft would allow Netscape to capitalize on a smaller opportunity. Fail to back down, and Microsoft would crush Netscape. Netscape wasn't interested in striking a deal. The conditions Microsoft proposed were illogical and ridiculous. The internet war was on.

The conversations between Microsoft and Netscape began innocently enough, dealing with technical standards issues and possible collaborative efforts. In a June 21, 1995, meeting,

Microsoft execs floated a truce that had all the earmarks of a threat: if Netscape declined to compete with Microsoft over the Windows 95 browser, Microsoft would allow Netscape to continue creating browser versions for other, less popular, platforms. Agree to Microsoft's wishes, and Microsoft would allow Netscape to capitalize on a smaller opportunity.[13] Fail to back down, and Microsoft would crush Netscape. Netscape wasn't interested in striking a deal. The conditions Microsoft proposed were illogical and ridiculous. The internet war was on.

Browser Brouhaha

After Netscape Navigator emerged as an early favorite, Microsoft scrambled for its own browser, making the same play it had with PC-DOS—license a program for cheap from another company, and exploit their effort in order to make huge gains. But it's a lot easier to fool companies when you're privately owned and still relatively unknown, and not a company with $6 billion in yearly revenue.

The browser was called Internet Explorer, a version of Mosaic that was developed by an Illinois-based software company called Spyglass, Inc. As part of the licensing deal, Microsoft agreed to pay Spyglass a quarterly payment and a percentage of royalties earned by Internet Explorer. Spyglass expected to make a killing on the deal. But instead of selling individual copies, Microsoft included Explorer with its *Internet Jumpstart Kit* for Windows 95 before giving it away later that year with Windows NT—meaning Spyglass wasn't recouping any royalty fees. Spyglass sued Microsoft, and the sides reached an agreement in early 1997, with Microsoft agreeing to pay $8 million to Spyglass.[14]

Spyglass CEO Doug Colbeth didn't hold back in discussing Microsoft's tactics to the *Chicago Sun-Times* in 1999. "You have to be willing to do some really painful things when you get hit by a factor of magnitude like Microsoft. Agility in our business is critical. If you're not agile, you're dead. There has to be an absolute stubbornness and commitment that you're not going to go into the Microsoft graveyard, and in order to stay out of the graveyard, you have to be willing to change your company," he said.[15]

Colbeth also expressed his view that Microsoft wasn't innovative—just forceful. "I'd like to have $3 billion [Microsoft's annual research budget]. I think we could innovate some additional things," he said. "What they are is a distribution company [and] a very good marketing company. When they see a good idea, they grab it, they buy it, they own it, they license it and then they distribute it better than anyone else in the world."

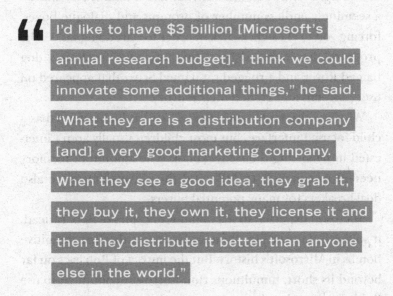

" I'd like to have $3 billion [Microsoft's annual research budget]. I think we could innovate some additional things," he said. "What they are is a distribution company [and] a very good marketing company. When they see a good idea, they grab it, they buy it, they own it, they license it and then they distribute it better than anyone else in the world."

Home and Away

The World Wide Web wasn't the only misfire from Microsoft in 1995. Microsoft wanted to bring a comforting approach to home computing, to make computer usage feel more like your living room than a screen full of files and programs and documents. So on March 31, 1995, Microsoft released its "social interface," named Bob.

With Microsoft Bob, users could enter different rooms and click icons corresponding with programs such as Letter Writer, Calendar, Checkbook, E-Mail, and a GeoSafari quiz game. Two Stanford University professors, Clifford Nass and Byron Reeves, with expertise in human-machine interactions, helped in Bob's development. Microsoft saw Bob as "friendly, approachable and fun,"[16] and its logo showed a smiley face wearing glasses. But customers instead found Bob to be clunky, cumbersome, and confusing. While Bob didn't include a user manual, it featured a seemingly endless number of prompts and dialogue boxes, forcing you to click-click-click in order to start doing tasks. The program also included "personal assistants" such as a dog named Rover and a rugged rat named Scuzz that appeared on users' screens and guided their journey.

Who was the target audience of Bob? It had potential as a child-focused interface, but most children usually aren't interested in balancing their checkbook. The amount of memory needed to run Bob (8 MB) and the price ($99) were also deal-breakers for many potential buyers.

Microsoft expected to sell millions of copies of Bob. Instead, it sold a little over fifty thousand—one of the first definitive bombs in Microsoft's history. But the impact of Bob lives on far beyond its short, tumultuous run. Microsoft continued to use Bob's "personal assistants" concept in ensuing program releases such as Microsoft Word—but instead of Rover or Scuzz, the company featured a new on-screen helper, an anamorphic paper clip nicknamed "Clippy."

The paper clip—its actual name is Clippit—first appeared in Office 97.[17] It would pop up with frustrating, usually unnecessary suggestions: "It looks like you're writing a letter. Would you like help?" You could ask it questions, and if you clicked on Clippy with your mouse, it would dance and roll its eyes and bend into different shapes. Users hated Clippy. It was a know-it-all, and obtrusive, and needy, and what the heck was it doing bending and flexing in the corner of your screen? With the release of Office XP, Microsoft finally recognized Clippy had to go, so the company created a campaign around Clippy's departure, including a poll about what Clippy should do with its newfound free time, and a series of videos in which Clippy, voiced by comedian Gilbert Gottfried, drinks its way through unemployment and endures family fights after losing its job.[18] Clippy's pain was real. And so was ours.

Another legacy of Bob that would appear in future Microsoft products: the much-derided font Comic Sans, developed by Microsoft designer Vincent Connare to reflect a child-oriented typeface.

Jokes and Jokes and Jokes

Microsoft also learned how to poke fun at itself every once and again. The *MicroNews*, the internal newsletter developed by former communications staffer Mario Juarez, would publish an April Fool's issue, littering articles with "Easter Eggs" and inside jokes about company policies, projects, and personnel, bringing a madcap *Mad* magazine presence to the company. "I had a group of friends that I knew from my earliest days in the company who had wicked senses of humor. So we would toss ideas around and I would spend the whole year writing it," Juarez said.

One of Juarez's bits involved things going horribly wrong with Microsoft's research labs. One year the story centered on Nathan Myrhvold, the company's research guru, being cryogenically frozen in Building 17 to be preserved to battle invaders from the future. "They used to say, 'People are our most important asset' . . . the company was making so much money that we wrote an article that said 'cash surpasses people as Microsoft's most important asset,'" Juarez said, laughing. There was also a joke about the company using hemp-based paper products for packaging that featured a photo of "product testers"—college students smoking weed on a couch.

"We got away with that stuff. And it was something that I think was reflective of an attitude of confidence and kind of a wicked joy that people were taking in the Microsoft experience," Juarez said. "At the time, I remember thinking, 'I can't believe I'm getting away with this.'"

Branching Out

By the mid-1990s, Microsoft needed new opponents—it had largely vanquished its rivals in the computer world. IBM was weak. Lotus was lost. Apple spiraled in the years after cofounder Steve Jobs's exit in the 1980s. Netscape was a potential threat due to its Navigator browser, but it wasn't seasoned or established enough to be considered a true rival.

As Microsoft reached new heights, it began branching outside of the PC world for the first time, forming partnerships and establishing brands in multimedia entertainment, news, and media—attempts to compete with emerging rivals such as AOL.

AOL, which began in the 1980s as an over-the-phone video game service called Control Video Corporation, gained traction in the early 1990s as a pay-based online service before shifting to dial-up internet.[19] AOL had one million members in 1995, and that number exploded to five million the next year. AOL offered a portal to the internet—a pipeline to shopping, sports, business, news, and information.

To challenge AOL, Microsoft launched the dial-up internet service The Microsoft Network (MSN). The Microsoft Network was paired with Windows 95, and MSN.com became a popular website full of links and information.

DreamWorks Interactive—a partnership with DreamWorks SKG, the entertainment company established by Steven Spielberg, Jeffrey Katzenberg, and David Geffen—provided Microsoft a path into the entertainment world, with a focus on adventure games, interactive stories, and family-oriented entertainment (Paul Allen, Microsoft's cofounder, invested $500 million in DreamWorks SKG).[20]

Despite the star power, DreamWorks Interactive fell flat, an imperfect mix of computer and entertainment forces. One computer game in particular, *Trespasser*, reflected the company's lofty ambitions and lackluster returns. *Trespasser* was seen as a digital sequel to the second *Jurassic Park* movie, *Lost World*. The game featured voice-overs from Sir Richard Attenborough and Minnie Driver and ran on a physics-based engine.

Video game designer Jonathan "Seamus" Blackley served as the executive producer of *Trespasser*, which was supposed to be released in 1997—the game's budget was connected to a deal DreamWorks had reached with a chip manufacturer. So the development was rushed, and the game's technology wasn't perfected before it was released to the world in 1998.[21]

The game was a bomb, full of glitches and pixelated graphics. The lead character's disembodied arm bent and twisted awkwardly, and players struggled to aim and fire weapons. "Sometimes extinction is the best thing," *Maximum PC* wrote. "Years in the making, *Trespasser* was to be the crowning achievement of realtime software terrain rendering, uniting an uber-realistic physics engine with a first-person adventure filled with detail. DreamWorks got the physics engine right, but the graphics and interface are horrid."[22]

But Gates was impressed by Blackley's efforts on the game and his physics background. He saw something in Blackley. Maybe he could be a good addition at Microsoft . . .

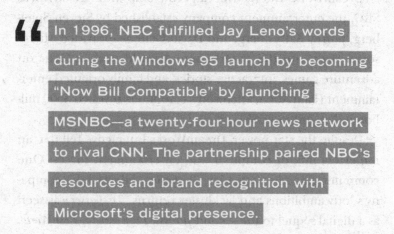

In 1996, NBC fulfilled Jay Leno's words during the Windows 95 launch by becoming "Now Bill Compatible" by launching MSNBC—a twenty-four-hour news network to rival CNN. The partnership paired NBC's resources and brand recognition with Microsoft's digital presence.

In 1996, NBC fulfilled Jay Leno's words during the Windows 95 launch by becoming "Now Bill Compatible" by launching MSNBC—a twenty-four-hour news network to rival CNN. The partnership paired NBC's resources and brand recognition with Microsoft's digital presence. Other Microsoft-backed media outlets, the online magazine *Slate* and WebTV, a TV-based web service, also launched in the mid-1990s.

Apple of Bill's Eye

Apple had fallen on tough times. But here was its cofounder Steve Jobs back onstage at Macworld 1997, getting a standing ovation. Jobs returned to Apple as an adviser after Gil Amelio was ousted as CEO, and he stressed the need for collaboration. Apple was in trouble and it needed all the help it could get— even if that help came from curious places. "Relationships that are destructive don't help anybody in this industry as it is to-day," he said.

As Jobs preached his message of burying the hatchet, a sur-prising face appeared on a video link to address the audience— Bill Gates.

Bill Gates?!

While Gates and Jobs famously shared the stage before, such as ahead of the Macintosh launch in 1984, there was a lot of bad blood between the companies in the ensuing years. Two years earlier, Jobs railed against Microsoft, claiming the tech giant had "no taste."[23]

"The only problem with Microsoft is they just have no taste, they have absolutely no taste, and what that means is—I don't mean that in a small way [,] I mean that in a big way. In the sense that they don't think of original ideas and they don't bring much culture into their product and you say why is that important—well you know proportionally spaced fonts come from type setting and beautiful books, that's where one gets the idea—if it weren't for the Mac they would never have that in their products and so I guess I am saddened, not by Microsoft's success—I have no problem with their success, they've earned their success for the most part. I have a problem with the fact that they just make really third-rate products."

But in 1997, Jobs was singing a different tune. Microsoft invested $150 million in Apple, and the companies announced a cease-fire on patent disputes, a commitment to releasing Office versions on Apple, and Apple deciding on Internet Explorer as its default browser. The crowd reacted to the announcements, and Gates's appearance, with a smattering of gasps and boos.

"We think Apple makes a huge contribution to the computer industry. We think it's going to be a lot of fun helping out," Gates said.

A world without rivals, even friendly ones, isn't a fun one. And as Jobs discussed years later, one of the companies didn't need to lose for the other to win. Microsoft's investment helped to stabilize Apple stock at a crucial time. Two decades later, the companies would be No. 1 and No. 2 in terms of market cap. Microsoft divested of its Apple shares by 2003. At that point, Jobs was firmly entrenched as Apple's chief executive and promoting the company's new online music store, iTunes. Microsoft launched an online music platform that year, too: MSN Radio Plus, which charged $4.99 a month for streaming, compared to Apple's per-song downloading charges.

Microsoft's 150,000 shares of preferred stock were converted to common stock—18.1 million shares—in 2001. If Microsoft held onto the stock through a 2005 stock split,[24] it would have had 36.2 million shares. Those 36.2 million shares would be worth $11.5 billion in 2020.

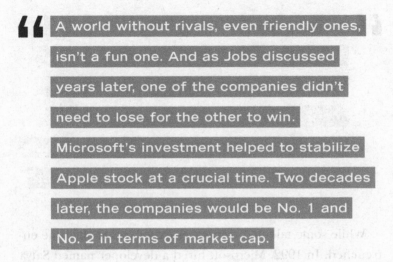

> A world without rivals, even friendly ones, isn't a fun one. And as Jobs discussed years later, one of the companies didn't need to lose for the other to win. Microsoft's investment helped to stabilize Apple stock at a crucial time. Two decades later, the companies would be No. 1 and No. 2 in terms of market cap.

Revolving Door

The 1990s marked a period of transition that saw Microsoft gain and lose talented employees. The workforce had grown to more than seventeen thousand by 1995. Gone were the days of Bill Gates being able to track employees' cars in the parking lot.

Many longtime employees became millionaires due to the success of the company's stock. And when money is no longer a concern, people often tend to pursue other passions and motives. Employees also left for new horizons and challenges—like, say, Amazon.com. Exec David Risher headed to the emerging online retailer in 1997—a move that Bill Gates told him would be "the stupidest decision you'll ever make" (actually, it wasn't—Risher made a fortune as one of Amazon's top executives and later cofounded Worldreader, a nonprofit devoted to providing the developing world with access to digital books).[25] Nathan Myhrvold, the founder of Microsoft's research division, departed the company to travel the world with his wife and sons.

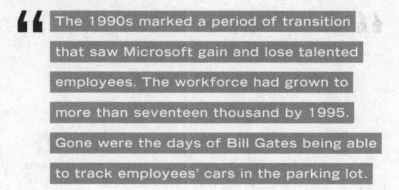

> The 1990s marked a period of transition that saw Microsoft gain and lose talented employees. The workforce had grown to more than seventeen thousand by 1995. Gone were the days of Bill Gates being able to track employees' cars in the parking lot.

While some talented employees exited, others became entrenched. In 1992, Microsoft hired a developer named Satya Nadella to join the Windows NT team and sell PCs to corporate buyers, aiding a group whose efforts would shape numerous Windows releases. Nadella, who grew up in India, the son of a civil servant father and Sanskrit scholar mother, adored one thing more than computers when he was a boy: cricket. But he was much better with computers than he was playing his favorite sport. His father bought him a computer when he was fifteen, a Sinclair ZX Spectrum computer kit.

"The ZX Spectrum inspired me to think about software, engineering, and even the idea that personal computing technologies could be democratizing," he wrote in his book, *Hit Refresh*. "If a kid in nowhere India could learn to program, surely anyone could."[26]

Nadella studied electrical engineering at Manipal Institute of Technology and later received a master's degree from the University of Wisconsin at Milwaukee. He became more proficient writing code and focused on theoretical computer science. Nadella worked at Sun Microsystems for two years before joining Microsoft. Nadella remembered the first time he met Steve Ballmer, the longtime exec. "He stopped by my office to give me one of his very expressive high fives for leaving Sun and joining Microsoft," Nadella wrote. "There was a true sense of mission and energy at the company then. The sky was the limit."

"Microsoft had a very wrong-headed approach to making friends in Washington, DC, and playing the influence game. We were terrible at it."

—NATHAN MYHRVOLD,
Former Chief Technology Officer at Microsoft

CROSSROADS

Attorney General Janet Reno wore a cream-colored suit, speaking firmly on May 18, 1998, as she outlined the Department of Justice's case against Microsoft. Reno's DOJ had gone after Microsoft earlier in the decade over its monopolistic practices and reached a settlement in 1994. But this was different—the federal government was joined by twenty states and the District of Columbia. The biggest issues tied back to Microsoft's handling of Windows 95, with requirements about Microsoft-based boot-up screens, its efforts to undermine Netscape, and forcing computer manufacturers to install Internet Explorer as a condition of getting Windows.

"Microsoft used its monopoly power to develop a choke-hold on the browser software needed to access the Internet," Reno said to a room full of video cameras and flashbulbs.

"Microsoft's actions have stifled competition in the operating system and browser markets. But most importantly, it has restricted the choices available for consumers in America and around the world.

"Today's action is intended to ensure that consumers and computer makers have the right to choose which software they want installed on their personal computers, and not have that software chosen for them. It is also designed to preserve competition and promote innovation in the computer software industry."[1] Reno, in a statement, said the DOJ wanted to "preserve competition and promote innovation."[2]

In its complaint, the government cited Gates's 1995 "Internet Tidal Wave" memo about the internet's rise, when he noted his desire to see Microsoft "match and beat" Netscape's offerings. By the time of the antitrust lawsuit, Microsoft had a 95 percent share of the PC operating system market. The remaining share belonged to IBM's OS/2, Unix, and other providers.

While Microsoft was building up market share, it was neglecting another key area of focus. "Microsoft had a very wrongheaded approach to making friends in Washington, DC, and playing the influence game," said former Chief Technology Officer Nathan Myhrvold. "We were terrible at it, and sadly, I noticed that before most other people did. So there's a whole bunch of memos on that and I didn't get listened to. So it was frustrating for me because I could see the whole thing as this slow-motion train wreck that was happening. Then I was trying as hard as I could to help."[3]

$1 Million a Day

The government's focus on Microsoft had intensified months earlier, in October 1997, when the Justice Department—believing Microsoft was in contempt of its 1995 consent decree about anti-competitive practices—urged a federal district court to fine the company $1 million a day until it stopped requiring PC manufacturers to preinstall Internet Explorer as a condition of licensing Windows 95, to ensure that Windows 95 functioned properly without Internet Explorer, and that easy instructions were provided on how to remove the Internet Explorer icon from the desktop.[4]

US District Judge Thomas Penfield Jackson heard arguments in December 1997 and issued an injunction calling for the company to separate Internet Explorer and Windows. Microsoft, issuing a public response to the injunction on December 15, offered PC makers two options: license a nonfunctional version of Windows, or one that was out of date.[5]

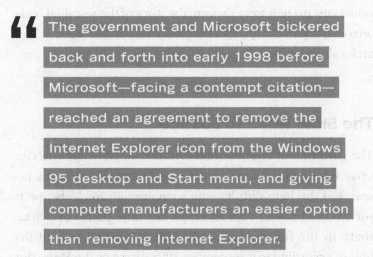

" The government and Microsoft bickered back and forth into early 1998 before Microsoft—facing a contempt citation— reached an agreement to remove the Internet Explorer icon from the Windows 95 desktop and Start menu, and giving computer manufacturers an easier option than removing Internet Explorer.

The government and Microsoft bickered back and forth into early 1998 before Microsoft—facing a contempt citation— reached an agreement to remove the Internet Explorer icon from the Windows 95 desktop and Start menu, and giving computer manufacturers an easier option than removing Internet Explorer. As the government built its case, Microsoft forged ahead with Windows 98 without consulting the court. An appeals court ruled that the injunction shouldn't apply to Windows 98.[6]

Pie on His Face

Bill Gates was arriving for a meeting in Belgium on February 4, 1998. He stepped out of the vehicle, smiled, and waved to on-lookers. As he walked up the steps to enter the building, he was pelted by a pie to the face.

Gates cowered and shook. Handlers came to his aid. Additional custard pies were thrown, the work of the so-called "cake terrorist," Noël Godin, and his group—an attack "against hier-archical power itself."[7]

The Slow Road to Justice

The government's fight was sweet justice for Netscape—its con-cerns were being taken seriously and Microsoft was in the hot seat. But the help didn't come soon enough for Netscape to survive the browser war. Netscape lost nine points of market share in the first half of 1998, while Microsoft gained five points, according to a September 1998 survey by the Massachu-setts company International Data Corporation. "The results of this third IDC survey tracking Web browser market share show a dramatic shift toward Microsoft Internet Explorer by midyear 1998. It appears that Microsoft's current battle with the US gov-ernment and Netscape's software giveaway have had little effect in keeping Netscape's market share from eroding," Joan-Carol Brigham with IDC said in a statement.[8]

Microsoft made progress across every segment and demographic while Netscape tanked with small business users. One area that was soft for Microsoft: medium and large businesses. "This is clearly a Netscape opportunity," Brigham said.

While it's easy to credit Microsoft alone with diminishing Netscape's market share, numerous factors were at play. The company struggled to build off of its success with Navigator, failing to roll out a second successful project, and scrapped planned development plans.

"Netscape was a classic example of a competitor, and Microsoft understood what to do about that—go out there and make a product that beats them in every way and just keep pushing them and keep pushing them," Nathan Myhrvold said.[9] "And over time you hope that, like Excel and Lotus 1-2-3, you win. So that notion of the way we win is we copy somebody else, we copy their strategy, we just out-execute them, was very ingrained in the company. And so that made it very difficult to go, and do things that other people weren't doing. So in a sense Netscape was maybe the last of the traditional competitors Microsoft had over the years."

Deflect, Deflect, Deflect

Gates smirked, and adjusted his glasses, and rolled his eyes, and rocked in his swivel chair, as he acted confused about the definition of words like *we* and *definition*. His deposition lasted for twenty hours spread across three days. And it was Gates at his most backhanded and belittling, the petty behavior that had grated on many of his employees. Gates, when questioned by

David Boies, the Justice Department's lead lawyer in the case, feigned ignorance about conversations he had, struggled when asked about the definition of API, stated he didn't understand numerous questions, and grappled with the definition of worlds like *we*.[10]

The behavior came from the man who could memorize paragraphs of code in his mind and synthesize dense reports at the same time he carried on conversations, the same guy who outsmarted Apple and IBM in turning his company into a superpower.

When video snippets of Gates's deposition were played in court, the judge shook his head and laughed, later calling his behavior "troubling." Some of Gates's key quotes from his deposition:[11]

- "You don't seem to like the facts!"
- "I don't know"—in some form, two hundred times.
- "If you define 'definition' for this conversation in a loose way, then I'll understand what you mean."
- "Our risk of being put out of business has been a constant feeling for me ever since we've been in business."

The videos remain popular online decades later—a notable lowlight in Gates's career.

In addition to Gates's shenanigans, Microsoft submitted falsified or inaccurate videos into evidence suggesting removing Internet Explorer from Windows caused malfunctions, or showing an overly simplified process for installing Netscape and adding the icon on a user's desktop.

Microsoft didn't take the threat of the lawsuit seriously. What was the government actually going to do?

"Cut Off Netscape's Air Supply"

The case brought troubling internal emails and conversations involving Microsoft to the forefront, revealing a flawed sense of immaturity and entitlement for the company. Intel VP Steven McGeady testified that Microsoft exec Paul Maritz, during a 1995 meeting, told Intel employees that Microsoft would "cut off Netscape's air supply" through its free browser software (Maritz has denied McGeady's claims).[12]

Internal Microsoft emails obtained by the government revealed the giant's true plans for Netscape. In a May 31, 1995, email to top company execs, Gates wrote, "I think there is a very powerful deal of some kind we can do with Netscape."[13] Gates's framework includes standards he wished to establish for the internet, as well as things he wished to avoid: open-source.

Gates suggested "servers will make money," and floated the possibility of helping Netscape with servers for twenty-four months "without hurting ourselves in any large way." In June 1995, after Microsoft brass met with Netscape executives, Gates weighed in on "the whole browser fight."

"The problem is that their strength comes from their [browser's] popularity and we have decided to make our own browser popular hard core. . . . This whole browser fight is going to be interesting. Their ambition to make money on browsers will hurt them. It's just a case of getting greedy. They are the ones who made the rules that browsers are free."

In a January 5, 1996, email, titled "OEMs and the Internet,"[14] Gates outlined Microsoft's browser goals. "Winning Internet browser share is a very very important goal for us," he wrote.

"I would like to understand what we need to do to convince OEMS to focus on our browser. . . . Promoting our Internet 2.0 browser to Oems and helping them see our commitment to leadership is very important." Days after that email, Gates talked with AOL CEO Steve Case, trying to pitch an AOL-Microsoft partnership.

"I told him I wanted to convince him to pay a visit and really talk about our goals. I said I wasn't going to be able to put AOL in the Windows box except in the sense that with a few strings typed in the user would be able to connect to AOL," Gates wrote in an email.

On April 10, 1996, Gates sent a long missive: "The Internet PC."[15]

"Microsoft's approach is to make Windows so Internet-friendly that no one using it will want a separate browser—not even a free browser. In Microsoft's view, people will use Windows to browse the web, just as they already use it to 'browse' servers on corporate networks or files on local disks."

Gates sent an email to his colleagues on May 19, 1996, following his "think week"—his escapes to a lake cabin to read and ponder the world's biggest problems. He labeled one section of the email "Browser war."

"If we continue to have minimal share in browsers a lot of our other efforts will be futile," he wrote. "By the end of the year we have to get to more than 25 percent share so we are taken seriously."

Antitrust Trial

The trial began on October 19, 1998—bringing Microsoft's practices into the open.

Boies, the Justice Department's lead lawyer in the case, used his opening remarks to shred, dice, and puree Gates's stances that Microsoft wasn't worried about Netscape's business, matching Gates's deposition video with emails showing a completely different approach—the raw, ruthless desire to destroy.

Among the evidence Boies presented was a memo Gates wrote to Microsoft exec Paul Maritz about his concerns competing against Netscape. "But in the meantime we can help them. We can pay them some money," he wrote.[16] Another key focal point was the June 1995 meeting in which Microsoft proposed dividing the internet software market. Gates, interviewed on video, denied suggesting the illegal offer. He didn't attend the meeting. Gates was also asked about investing in Netscape but said he disagreed.

Internal memos suggested the opposite. "I think there is a very powerful deal of some kind we can do with Netscape," Gates wrote in the May 31, 1995, message.

"The concept is that for 24 months they agree to do certain things in the client and we agree to help make their server business successful. . . . This kind of deal could be a big win-win. Of course over time we will compete on servers but we can help them a lot in the meantime. We could even pay them money as part of the deal buying some piece of them or something. I would really like to see something like this happen!!"

Microsoft lawyer John Warden tried to suggest his company was in fact the underdog. "Netscape had what the government would consider a monopoly in the market for Internet browsers until the great Satan, Microsoft, came along," Warden said sarcastically during his opening remarks.[17] And instead of viewing Internet Explorer as an add-on such as a camera flash or car radio, Microsoft compared it to "a shutter on a camera or a car's transmission."

The June 1995 Communication

Netscape CEO James Barksdale wrote in written testimony that Microsoft execs promised a "special relationship" in that June 1995 meeting—if Netscape agreed not to compete against Windows 95.[18]

Microsoft had good reason to develop a "special relationship" with Netscape. By Q2 in 1995, Netscape had generated $10 million in revenue by its browser, and that revenue spiked to $45 million by the end of the year. Additionally, Netscape reached deals with computer manufacturers to install Navigator.

Barksdale recalled the tone of the conversations changing during the June 21, 1995, meeting. "Microsoft proposed a division of the browser market between our companies: if Netscape would agree not to produce a Windows 95 browser that would compete with Internet Explorer, Microsoft would 'allow' Netscape to continue to produce cross-platform versions of its browser for the relatively small market of non-Windows 95 platforms: namely, Windows 3.1, Macintosh, and Unix. Moreover, Microsoft made clear that if Netscape did not agree to its plan to divide the browser market, Microsoft would crush Netscape, using its operating system monopoly, by freely incorporating all of the functionality of Netscape's products into Windows," Barksdale wrote in his testimony.[19]

Additionally, according to Barksdale, Microsoft staffers discussed the tech specifications that would allow Netscape to run with Windows 95—and how getting the tech assistance would be easier if Netscape agreed to Microsoft's plans.

"I left the meeting stunned that Microsoft had made such an explicit proposal. And I was surprised at the degree of threat to the Windows monopoly apparently perceived by Microsoft, especially because [the] Internet Explorer product had not yet even been introduced and would not be introduced until after the release of Windows 95," Barksdale wrote. "Moreover, Netscape Navigator was a software application with platform characteristics, but it was not an operating system, like Windows. Given these facts, Microsoft could only have had one goal: to obtain and control a significant proportion of the future growth of the Internet."[20]

Barksdale's concerns became realized after Microsoft began bundling the free versions of Internet Explorer with Windows in December 1995, sending Netscape's stock tumbling. Microsoft further used free add-ons, and occasionally financial payments, for copies of Navigator removed and replaced with Internet Explorer, Barksdale alleged. "It was impossible to stay competitive with 'better than free,'" he wrote.

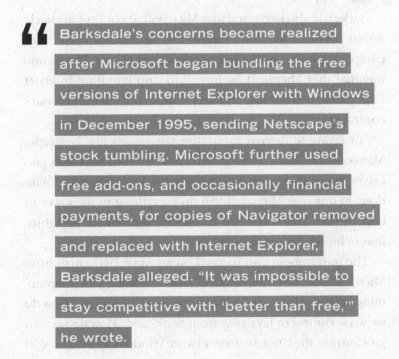

Barksdale's concerns became realized after Microsoft began bundling the free versions of Internet Explorer with Windows in December 1995, sending Netscape's stock tumbling. Microsoft further used free add-ons, and occasionally financial payments, for copies of Navigator removed and replaced with Internet Explorer, Barksdale alleged. "It was impossible to stay competitive with 'better than free,'" he wrote.

Barksdale also suggested that Microsoft would pressure computer manufacturers such as Compaq that planned to install Netscape Navigator over Internet Explorer, threatening to pull their Windows licenses, "which would have put them out of business."

Barksdale summarized his frustrations with Microsoft as such: "I understand the pushes and pulls of competitive marketplaces; I understand that bullying and tough tactics do not necessarily violate any laws. But I also understand monopoly power and how it can be abused. My first job was as a salesman for IBM, and I learned there through rigorous sales training that there is a legal limit, a place where bullying and tough tactics by a monopolist cross a line that should not and cannot be crossed. It is my view, based on what I have experienced and seen in the last several years, that Microsoft's behaviors have crossed that line."[21]

Barksdale also suggested that Microsoft, if not kept in check, would continue to stifle industry innovation and keep other companies from developing products out of fear. He recommended that Microsoft be forced to stop bundling Internet Explorer and Windows, and be prohibited from exclusionary contracts.

"By trying to destroy innovative companies like Netscape, Microsoft has sent a message to the industry—if Microsoft perceives that your success has the potential to undermine Windows in any way, Microsoft will do everything in its power to destroy you. The end result is reduced innovation, and thus, fewer choices for consumers."

The government also focused on an April 1997 email from Microsoft executive Ben Slivka to Gates involving Java programming language in which he listed questions, including, "How do we wrest control of Java away from Sun?" and "How do we turn Java into just the latest, best way to write Windows applications?"[22]

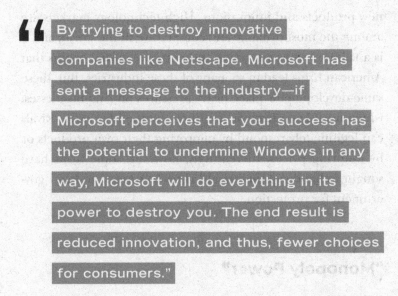

" By trying to destroy innovative companies like Netscape, Microsoft has sent a message to the industry—if Microsoft perceives that your success has the potential to undermine Windows in any way, Microsoft will do everything in its power to destroy you. The end result is reduced innovation, and thus, fewer choices for consumers."

"Out to Destroy Microsoft"

Microsoft was getting hammered in the court of public opinion—and Bill Gates, the face of the company, was tired of it. Gates, speaking to reporters on a video link in December 1998, erupted, accusing the government's lead attorney, David Boies, of being "really out to destroy Microsoft . . . really out to take all the good work we've done and make us look very bad."[23]

The company tried unsuccessfully to spin the narrative. On June 2, 1999, full-page ads for the Independent Institute were published in the *New York Times* and *Washington Post* under the headline "An Open Letter to President Clinton from 240 Economists on Antitrust Protectionism."

"Consumers did not ask for these antitrust actions—rival business firms did. Consumers of high technology have enjoyed falling prices, expanding outputs, and a breathtaking array of new products and innovations. High technology markets are among the most dynamic and competitive in the world, and it is a tribute to open markets and entrepreneurial genius that American firms lead in so many of these industries. But, these same developments place heavy pressures on rival businesses, which must keep pace or lose their competitive races. Rivals can legitimately respond by improving their own products or by lowering prices. Increasingly, however, some firms have sought to handicap their rivals' races by turning to [the] government for protection."

"Monopoly Power"

Judge Jackson, on November 5, 1999, released a 207-page "findings of fact" that outlined Microsoft's monopolistic practices and the case ahead.[24]

For one, Microsoft could charge whatever price it liked, "for a significant period of time without losing an unacceptable amount of business to competitors."

Jackson outlined numerous factors that revealed Microsoft's "monopoly power," including:

1. Market share for Intel-compatible PC operating systems well above 90 percent.
2. An applications barrier prevented other companies from entering the marketplace—and many applications were written specifically for Windows. Windows' popularity was self-fueling, a "positive feedback loop" for Microsoft that served as a "vicious cycle" for competitors. And Microsoft's success left customers with few viable options.

3. Microsoft focusing its energy on guarding against "Middleware" threats such as Netscape Navigator and Java.

To highlight his point, the judge pointed to IBM's OS/2 Wrap, which gained only 10 percent of the PC market after its 1994 release. Amid the widespread success of Windows 95, IBM focused on niche markets, mostly banks, because Windows had sucked up so much of the company's opportunity. Apple's Mac OS was also cited—even Apple's efforts didn't do much to chip away at Microsoft's market share. Nothing could.

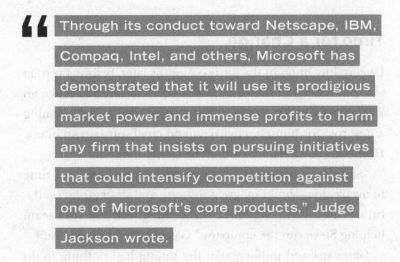

> Through its conduct toward Netscape, IBM, Compaq, Intel, and others, Microsoft has demonstrated that it will use its prodigious market power and immense profits to harm any firm that insists on pursuing initiatives that could intensify competition against one of Microsoft's core products," Judge Jackson wrote.

"Through its conduct toward Netscape, IBM, Compaq, Intel, and others, Microsoft has demonstrated that it will use its prodigious market power and immense profits to harm any firm that insists on pursuing initiatives that could intensify competition against one of Microsoft's core products," Judge Jackson wrote. "Microsoft's past success in hurting such companies and stifling innovation deters investment in technologies and businesses that exhibit the potential to threaten Microsoft. The ultimate result is that some innovations that would truly benefit consumers never occur for the sole reason that they do not coincide with Microsoft's self-interest."[25]

Jackson's fact-finding didn't come with a conclusion about Microsoft's conduct—but it all but promised that Microsoft would face the government's wrath. Would the judge break apart Microsoft? How would that new structure take shape? What would it mean for the PC industry? Was the government going to crush Microsoft the way the company had crushed its rivals?

Time for a Change

Uncertainty hung in the air two months later, before a verdict was announced in the case, as Bill Gates decided to make an announcement. He was stepping down as CEO—and assuming a new role for himself, chairman and chief software architect. His buddy Steve Ballmer would be taking the reins.

"Steve's promotion will allow me to dedicate myself full-time to my passion—building great software and strategizing on the future, and nurturing and collaborating with the core team helping Steve run the company," Gates said in a statement.[26]

Gates stressed publicly that the timing had nothing to do with the government's case against Microsoft, and that he wasn't concerned about the company potentially being broken up.

The truth was muddy. Things were less fun for Gates; the trial dominated everything. He snapped at people more than usual. Sometimes he got sappy or emotional in meetings. His company was getting picked apart by the government and Melinda was home caring for the kids and his reputation was being trashed and he was being pelted with pies, and things weren't so simple as they were when he and Paul Allen were writing a BASIC Interpreter for a machine they'd never used, two kids with heads full of dreams.

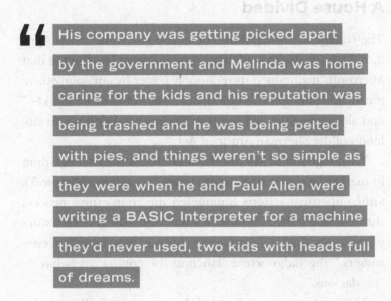

" His company was getting picked apart by the government and Melinda was home caring for the kids and his reputation was being trashed and he was being pelted with pies, and things weren't so simple as they were when he and Paul Allen were writing a BASIC Interpreter for a machine they'd never used, two kids with heads full of dreams.

"It was a very hard thing for Bill. You think you've done everything right and then all of a sudden you have all these people telling you that it's all wrong and you're terrible. It was very difficult," said Gates's friend and former Microsoft exec Nathan Myhrvold.[27]

If there was anyone ready to succeed Gates, it was Steve Ballmer, his trusty No. 2 for nearly two decades and one of the few people who could match Gates's intensity about Microsoft. Ballmer was an important part of Microsoft's success—many of the company's growth initiatives happened because of his input. Ballmer supplemented and reinforced Gates's vision and determination. Ballmer believed in Microsoft. But Ballmer wasn't

Gates. No one was. And Gates wasn't really *leaving*, and that complicated everything further.

A House Divided

The change at the top didn't deter the government. On April 3, 2000, Judge Jackson filed his conclusions of law, finding that Microsoft "maintained its monopoly power by anticompetitive means and attempted to monopolize the Web browser market," and also unlawfully tied Internet Explorer to Windows, in violation of the Sherman Antitrust Act.[28]

The judge found Microsoft did not break the law regarding its marketing arrangements with other companies. "Microsoft's anticompetitive actions trammeled the competitive process through which the computer software industry generally stimulates innovation and conduces to the optimum benefit of consumers," the judge wrote, labeling the company's behavior "predacious."

The punishment was handed down on June 7, 2000, and it was severe. Microsoft would be split in half—the first corporate antitrust breakup since 1984. One side of Microsoft would handle operating systems, while the other would handle applications. Microsoft unbundled. The order allowed Microsoft four months to come up with a plan for breaking up the company. Microsoft was also ordered to hand over API data to programmers, stop degrading the performance of non-Microsoft middleware, allow computer manufacturers to display whichever desktop program icons they wished, and establish a compliance committee of at least three members responsible for supervising Microsoft's processes to ensure compliance.

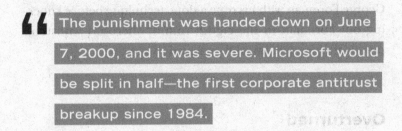

" The punishment was handed down on June 7, 2000, and it was severe. Microsoft would be split in half—the first corporate antitrust breakup since 1984.

"Microsoft as it is presently organized and led is unwilling to accept the notion that it broke the law or accede to an order amending its conduct," Judge Jackson wrote.

Jackson worried that without swift action, Microsoft's monopolistic behavior would continue, and noted that the company has been "untrustworthy."

The company's hostility and cavalier attitude, all of Gates's smugness, backfired. But just because Microsoft lost didn't mean it was surrendering. Gates called the decision "the beginning of a new chapter in this case."

"This is clearly the most massive attempt at government regulation of the technology industry ever, and it was conceived by the government and imposed by this ruling without a single day of testimony or scrutiny. This plan would undermine our high-tech economy, hurt consumers, make computers harder to use, and impact thousands of other companies and employees throughout the high-tech industry," Gates said.[29]

The message conveyed within the company: Microsoft was a victim, and the case was unfair, and the judge and prosecutor were out of control. At a 2000 company party celebrating Microsoft's twenty-fifth birthday, Ballmer popped out of a cake and aired a clip of boxer Muhammad Ali, representing Microsoft, during his famed 1974 "Rumble in the Jungle" fight in which Ali withstood punch after punch, tiring out

George Foreman with his rope-a-dope technique before knocking out Foreman in the eighth round. Microsoft withstood punch after punch, but still expected to win.

Overturned

Loose lips sink ships, so the saying goes, and Judge Jackson's loose lips helped keep Microsoft intact. Judge Jackson spoke to the media about the Microsoft case and didn't hold back.

"I think [Gates] has a Napoleonic concept of himself and his company, an arrogance that derives from power and unalloyed success, with no leavening hard experience, no reverses," he told the *New Yorker*. He said of Microsoft officials, "They don't act like grown-ups!"[30]

As Microsoft appealed the decision to split the company, the US Court of Appeals for the District of Columbia spent two days in February 2001 considering the case, rendering a decision on June 28, 2001.

The future of Microsoft hung in the balance. This was the company's last great chance to stay intact. The appeals court decided to reverse the ruling to split the company, in large part because of the judge's statements. "The system would be a sham if all judges went around doing this," said Harry Edwards, chief judge of the court of appeals.

Microsoft wanted the judge's findings vacated. That wouldn't happen. The ruling that Microsoft was relying on monopolistic practices remained. The company had to make some concessions. But Microsoft was remaining intact. Timing contributed to the outcome. The Clinton administration and Janet Reno left office in January 2001, replaced by Republican George W.

Bush and Attorney General John Ashcroft. The new administration didn't feel as strongly about pursuing the case.

On November 1, 2001, one day before a court-imposed deadline, Microsoft and the DOJ reached a settlement in which Microsoft would share its APIs with third-party companies and allow a three-party panel to have access to Microsoft's systems and processes for five years.

The grueling battle with the government begrudgingly taught Microsoft to play within the system instead of trying to overpower it. Microsoft's old model, one of brute force, would have to change. In the end, the case wasn't as much about antitrust as it was about a company that had misbehaved for so long—karmic retribution for years of ruthlessness. Microsoft began funneling money—lots and lots of money—into lobbying, exerting its influence in Washington to become "one of the most dominating, multifaceted, and sophisticated influence machines around," *Fortune* wrote in 2002. The government was a lot more likely to stay out of Microsoft's way if Microsoft was helping to begin, and end, the tough conversations.

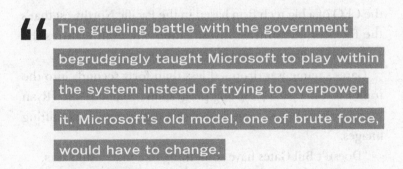

The grueling battle with the government begrudgingly taught Microsoft to play within the system instead of trying to overpower it. Microsoft's old model, one of brute force, would have to change.

Microsoft's interactions with the government and public skirmishes left the company exposed. Any other tech company could come along and follow Microsoft's blueprint—companies like Apple or Yahoo or a search engine named Google. The secrets weren't secret anymore. The superpower was weakened. And the tech world was constantly changing.

Not Quite Reality

Hollywood had a Bill Gates fixation. A 1999 made-for-TV movie, *Pirates of Silicon Valley,* detailed the rivalry between Gates (Anthony Michael Hall) and Apple's Steve Jobs (Noah Wyle). The movie captures the founders' intensity and drive, as well as accusations of intellectual theft that have circled both companies, such as Apple's using Xerox PARC technology as inspiration for the Lisa computer and Macintosh 128K released in 1983 and 1984.

Gates was asked about the movie in a 2013 Reddit AMA. "That portrayal was reasonably accurate," he wrote.

The 2001 movie *Antitrust,* meanwhile, stars Tim Robbins as a thinly veiled version of Gates named Gary Winston. Gary is the CEO of a big tech firm based in the Pacific Northwest that's the focus of an antitrust investigation. He even features the same part in his hair and rustic dad chic clothes as Gates.

Gates's name was dropped less than forty seconds into the trailer, as Gary shows a young programmer named Milo (Ryan Phillippe) his home, complete with a digital canvas of shifting images.

"Doesn't Bill Gates have something like that?" Milo asks.

"Bill who?"

But where Gates was emphatic about capturing the browser market, Gary is all about a different kind of control—surveilling employees, stealing their code, and having them murdered.

Critics and film audiences treated *Antitrust* like it was the OS/2 operating system—it was criticized and largely ignored, and then it went away. The *Chicago Tribune* called the movie "a big techno-dud."

"When Microsoft bought Bungee, Steve Jobs called up Bill Gates, and I think Ed Fries had to take the call. Steve was irate."

—DEAN TAKAHASHI,
Longtime Video Game Journalist

INTO YOUR LIVING ROOM

Microsoft's new battle didn't involve operating systems or web browsers, it involved video games—a shift to the living room. Video games was one area where Microsoft found scattered success but didn't dominate. MS-DOS was a platform for PC gaming, and Microsoft had a popular flight simulator program. But amid the Windows 95 launch, high-performance multimedia was a concern, and DirectX was born, a collection of APIs (Application Programming Interfaces) to handle games and other multimedia.

The video game console and PC worlds were converging, led by Sony's PlayStation, a home entertainment gaming system that played CDs. A follow-up, PlayStation 2, was scheduled for release in 2000, and it was going to further disrupt the PC gaming industry.

Microsoft had to do something . . .

Enter Seamus Blackley, the video game developer from DreamWorks Interactive who'd served as executive producer of the clunky *Jurassic Park* PC game *Trespasser* with the glitches and pixelated graphics. Gates recruited him to join Microsoft in February 1999, and he teamed with three other employees to develop a way to compete against Sony: Kevin Bachus, Ted Hase, and Otto Berkes.[1] The initial plan for the DirectX Box involved enlisting an outside company—maybe IBM or Dell or Fujitsu—to build hardware to run PC games. But computer makers weren't keen on building a machine since the real money came from the actual video games, not the hardware. And the market wasn't interested in a video game machine running PC games.

Microsoft would have to create a video game system itself. Production was outsourced to the multinational firm Flextronics, and the name of the console was shortened from DirectX Box to Xbox.

Microsoft focused on electronic storage for its Xbox—8 gigabytes (later models had 10 GB). PlayStation 2, for comparison's sake, relied on 8 MB memory cards. But storage is expensive. The system was going to cost Microsoft more than the $299 price point. But the real payoff in video game systems is the software, not the hardware—and in order to establish itself and stand beside Sony, Microsoft would have to take a financial hit.

Microsoft devoted one thousand employees to Xbox and situated them in a building a few miles away from the company's main campus. The new branch campus took on a different attitude, reflecting Microsoft's fun, looser side.

Blackley and other executives like Ed Fries, Microsoft's VP of games publishing, brought deep video game connections and authenticity, something that couldn't be purchased, to the project. The Xbox had potential. But it needed its own "killer app." It needed a standout game. Microsoft struggled to reach deals with Japanese developers. Sony's shadow loomed large, and the company also faced cultural and language barriers.

Maybe there were development opportunities stateside . . .

A Coveted Game

Steve Jobs glided across the stage, excitement pouring out of him as he discussed upcoming projects. It was the Macworld conference in New York, July 21, 1999. Jobs—clad in his iconic black turtleneck with the sleeves rolled up, a face full of stubble and a pair of jeans—was back with Apple as iCEO, "interim" CEO. The presentation reached its apex when Jobs discussed video games. One in particular, from Illinois-based developer Bungie, stood above the rest.[2]

"We are starting to see some great games come back to the Mac, but this is one of the coolest I've ever seen," Jobs said, beaming. "This game is gonna ship early next year from Bungie, and this is the first time anybody has ever seen it—it's the first time they've debuted it."

Jobs invited Jason Jones, Bungie's cofounder, to the stage. "*Halo* is the name of this game. And we're gonna see, for the first time, *Halo*," Jobs said.

Jones played a clip showing futuristic fighters battling aliens on a faraway planet, driving a warthog across a desert landscape, the fighters jostling around during their ride. Sunlight glimmers and reflects off of objects. Orchestral music plays underneath the action. The game, set hundreds of years in the future, centers on a group of humans facing a brutal war against aliens known as the Covenant. The surviving humans wind up battling the Covenant on a giant ringed system that features a breathable atmosphere—a Halo. Development of the game began in 1997. It was initially conceived as a strategy game, and later a third-person shooter.

The game was stunning and significant. An extended clip from the game was shown at the E3 Conference in June 2000, again wowing its viewers. Microsoft had seen enough. It needed to have *Halo*, so it ended up acquiring Bungie.

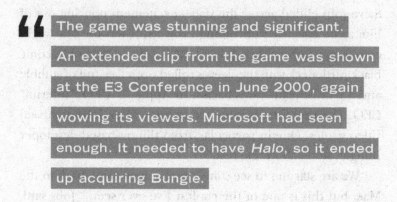

> The game was stunning and significant. An extended clip from the game was shown at the E3 Conference in June 2000, again wowing its viewers. Microsoft had seen enough. It needed to have *Halo*, so it ended up acquiring Bungie.

"When Microsoft bought Bungie, Steve Jobs called up Bill Gates, and I think Ed Fries had to take the call. Steve was irate that they had stolen away Bungie," said longtime video game journalist Dean Takahashi. Microsoft ended up agreeing to "porting of games to the Macintosh to make good on this whole deal," a way for Jobs to try and save face.[3]

Apple could be as angry as it wanted, but Microsoft simply recognized an opportunity and took advantage of it. Bungie founder and CEO Alexander Seropian saw potential in his company's partnership with Microsoft. "This is an opportunity to combine the strength of two outstanding software companies: Bungie's talent for creating great games and Microsoft's strength in distribution," Seropian said in a 2000 press release.[4] "Microsoft will provide us with the resources and infrastructure we need to continue to build great games and make them available on a worldwide scale. We are also looking forward to helping define the Xbox platform, which may soon be the world's premier game console."

Halo: Combat Evolved was released in November 2001 as a first-person shooter—an iconic release that redefined the potential of video games and gave the Xbox its first breakaway hit (PC and Mac OS versions were released in 2003). Attention to detail made *Halo* stand out. Spent shell casings litter the ground. It also benefits from the user's ability to imagine themselves as the main character, known as the Master Chief, whose helmeted face and armored body are never seen.

"Bungie did some great work in figuring out how to make a shooter work on a game controller in a way that was just much more fluid and accurate than had been done before," said Dean Takahashi.[5]

More than sixty million units and $4.6 billion in worldwide sales later (as well as a long-rumored movie that never came to fruition), *Halo* remains a staple for Xbox fans—the game that launched Microsoft's video game legacy.

Quality Above All

Microsoft had no way to catch PlayStation 2 at the onset—more than seventy-five million consoles had been sold. Instead of worrying about catching up, Microsoft could focus on making the Xbox unique and different and stellar.

Xbox featured an Intel 733-megahertz processor and an 8-gigabyte hard drive and was also internet compatible. After Xbox was announced, Sony adjusted—introducing a hard drive and internet connection for PlayStation 2. The price point of

PS2 was also adjusted, from $375 to $299. The video game console wars were on.

Microsoft lost a lot of money on the initial Xbox—nearly $1 billion.

The costs could have sunk lesser companies, but Microsoft had the resources to endure lean years. Other companies would have needed to come up with immediate gains. They wouldn't have been able to withstand or justify losing $100 or more on each console.

Microsoft's resources allowed the Xbox team to focus on innovation and quality—doing it right instead of simply doing it cheap. And doing it right would pay off in spades as Xbox's developers set out to follow up their initial offering.

The Xbox launched in November 2001. At the launch event, Seamus Blackley stood onstage with Bill Gates and Dwayne "The Rock" Johnson, the pro wrestler and acting star, wearing "illegal red" shoes—a color that wasn't visible on older television sets.

"This was a message to game developers, that we understand you and we know what you're like," tech journalist Dean Takahashi said. "They were the only ones who would get that."

Amid PlayStation 2's popularity and Xbox's launch, Nintendo had its own console released in 2001, the GameCube. Originally codenamed "Project Dolphin," the console focused on gaming only—it didn't play CDs or DVDs, only miniDVD-format discs. Nintendo was also family friendly, so it shied away from megahits like *Halo* or *Grand Theft Auto*, an open-world game series in which you travel around town committing crimes, eluding police, and completing shameful tasks.

Nintendo's GameCube wasn't a failure by any stretch. It sold more than twenty million units and featured familiar franchises such as Super Smash Bros. and Zelda. But it simply couldn't do as much as the PlayStation or Xbox. PlayStation and Xbox were different—computers that happened to play video games for your living room or bedroom.

Xbox Live

Connection was Microsoft's next big focus for Xbox growth—a chance for users to play others around the world while sitting in their own homes.

Xbox Live paired high-speed cable or DSL with high-energy *Halo* or *Call of Duty*. "While Sony and Nintendo have online plans, networked game playing is peripheral to their video-game strategies. For Microsoft, it has been integral to the Xbox plan from the beginning—the wedge with which Microsoft hopes to gain entry to the nation's and world's living rooms and become an entertainment powerhouse," the *New York Times* wrote in 2002.[6]

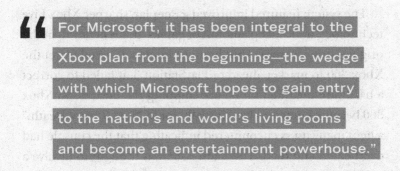

" For Microsoft, it has been integral to the Xbox plan from the beginning—the wedge with which Microsoft hopes to gain entry to the nation's and world's living rooms and become an entertainment powerhouse."

Users could download add-ons, build their achievements, and even mask their voice in the headset. The bet could have been a major bust—server space is expensive, and making consoles internet-ready drove up the cost. But Microsoft saw a way to bring in monthly payments from users looking for more out of their consoles.

Xbox Live had its early critics, namely Sony, which wondered whether Xbox Live would ever break even. "If I were Microsoft, I would spend my money first on selling units rather than building an online service," Kazuo Hirai, the president and chief operating officer of Sony Computer Entertainment America, said in 2002.[7]

The risk would eventually pay off for Microsoft to the tune of more than $1 billion a year.

A Costly Crisis

Microsoft wanted to win the console wars in 2005—and it ended up paying dearly. Microsoft prepared its follow-up to its initial Xbox with Xbox 360, so named because of the console's all-encompassing nature (that, and naming it Xbox 2 would make it appear a step behind PlayStation 3).

The system featured improved gameplay, sharper Xbox Live technology, and a deep amount of games. It was better than the original in many ways—but because Microsoft raced to get the Xbox 360 to market ahead of PlayStation 3, it failed to correct a hardware malfunction before shipping the devices. So Xbox 360 became known, at least initially, for its "Red Ring of Death," a light many users encountered indicating that the console had overheated and died. The main issue was thought to involve a switch to lead-free solder.

"The lead-free solder was environmentally a good idea, but not necessarily ready. And so when they put it onto the circuit boards and soldered in the CPU, they thought it would be fine.

But when there were certain heat conditions, it would come loose in its socket," said Dean Takahashi. Engineers recognized problems on the production line and suggested Microsoft stop and uncover the problem.

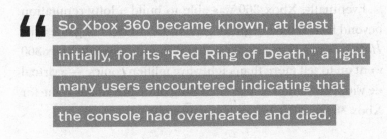

> So Xbox 360 became known, at least initially, for its "Red Ring of Death," a light many users encountered indicating that the console had overheated and died.

"The trains did not stop and Microsoft continued to try and stay on schedule and shop these machines. And when you have a high failure rate in the factory, that means the failure rate in the field is going to be high as well," Takahashi said.

It was a big problem for people who'd plunked down $299 or more. Microsoft, ever the software company, had gotten used to rolling out products then releasing fixes after the fact, as it had throughout the 1980s and 1990s, but the Xbox 360 problems dealt with hardware, not software. The console's failure rate was estimated at nearly 25 percent, far above the usual rate of about 5 percent.[8]

Microsoft prioritized deadlines over quality and paid dearly. As the problems mounted, Xbox exec Peter Moore calculated that it would cost $1.15 billion to fix the problem, and he discussed the issue with Ballmer.

"OK, talk me through this," Ballmer told Moore.

"If we don't do this, this brand is dead," Moore said. "This is a Tylenol moment," referring to a rash of drug tampering deaths in the early 1980s.

As the conversation continued, Moore recalled to IGN in 2011,[9] Ballmer asked what it would cost. Gulp.

"We think it's $1.15 billion, Steve," he said.

"Do it," Ballmer told him. No hesitation, no challenge, no fretting. If that's what it would cost, Microsoft would make it right.

Eventually, Xbox 360 was able to build a lofty reputation beyond its troubled beginnings. On the strength of games like *Halo 3, Grand Theft Auto V, Gears of War,* and *Minecraft,* Xbox 360 went on to sell more than eighty-five million copies[10]—a virtual tie with PlayStation 3. The "Red Ring of Death" finally came for Xbox 360 in 2016, but its legacy prevails.

The Future of Gaming . . . Sort Of

Microsoft wanted gamers to ditch their controllers. After Nintendo found success with its wand-guided Wii device, Microsoft was also looking at developing technology beyond the typical thumb-driven video game format.

The company spent years developing a project, codename Natal, that could track a player's movements through sensors and an infrared camera. The project was unveiled in 2010 with a new name: Kinect.

Suddenly, your living room became "a zoo, a stadium, a fitness room or a dance club," Kudo Tsunoda, creative director for Microsoft Game Studios, said at the time Kinect was announced. "You will be in the center of your entertainment, using the best controller ever made—you."[11]

Kinect was seen as Xbox's—and Microsoft's—future. A disruptor. A game changer.

It was released amid a wave of publicity, including an episode of Oprah Winfrey's TV show in which the host gave away

360s and Kinects to each audience member, causing the crowd to erupt in cheers and jump in disbelief.

Microsoft ended up selling eight million Kinect sensors in the product's first sixty days, netting a Guinness record for the fastest-selling consumer electronics device.[12] And games such as *Kinect Adventures*—which featured a player's avatar competing in adventures and other sports challenges—rank among the top-selling Xbox titles.

But Kinect failed to gain a major market share among Xbox users, and game developers were slow to make games that used the technology. Microsoft struggled to connect Kinect with the proper audience—the games were largely catered to families and children. Adding the Kinect technology, with its $149 initial price tag, pushed the price of the console ever higher. It could also be glitchy at times, especially with users who had less traditional body types, or pregnant women.

And then there was the security and privacy issue. Gamers bristled at the idea of allowing Microsoft to listen and watch in on all of their private moments. Microsoft tried to reassure its customers that their conversations are "not being recorded or uploaded." But Microsoft was always listening, awaiting the "Xbox On" command.

Kinect was a major part of the plans for Xbox's future, until it wasn't, and it was discontinued in 2017. It reflected a great effort that moved video gaming in a new direction, even if it fell short of its lofty expectations.

"All-in-One Entertainment System"

Xbox One, released in 2013, represented a shift away from the PowerPC-based architecture, Xenon processor, and "Red Ring of Death" of Xbox 360. Instead, it featured X86-based hardware like the PlayStation 4, the common hardware making it easier for game developers. It was seen as an "all-in-one entertainment system." Subsequent upgrades—Xbox One S in 2016, and Xbox One X in 2017—brought Xbox gaming to 4K and improved power to the console.

Backward compatibility, announced in 2015, marked a significant shift from the initial Xbox One release—then-Xbox head Don Mattrick trashed backward compatibility only two years earlier. "If you're backwards compatible, you're really backwards," he told the *Wall Street Journal*.[13]

Xbox started looking backward—and it propelled the console forward.

Game Pass

Welcome to the "Netflix of video games." Microsoft in 2017 launched Game Pass, a platform featuring hundreds of video game titles available to download and play. A PC version was released in 2019.

You start a new campaign of *Halo*, then bale hay in *Farming Simulator 17*, switch to the quirky battle simulator *TABS*, go trophy hunting in *The Hunter: Call of the Wild*, and finish your night playing *Supermarket Shriek*, an oddly refreshing game in which a man and goat, riding in a shopping cart, yell to propel themselves through different obstacle courses.

Game Pass is Microsoft's answer to PlayStation Now, which features a much larger library but has also been limited by tech issues. Many of the games in PlayStation Now could only be streamed, instead of downloaded, leading to diminished quality and glitches as you played them.

Xbox Game Pass also included all-new first-party titles—and seamless transfer between Xbox One and PC. And Game Pass, at less than $15 a month, comes in cheaper than PlayStation's $20.

Standout Xbox Games

Xbox is celebrated for its games—its gaming experience has consistently set it apart from PlayStation's releases. Here are some of the most notable games during Xbox's first two decades.

Halo franchise: *Halo* has remained an Xbox exclusive since 2001, and the game franchise has stayed with Microsoft even after its creator, Bungie, split from the company in 2007. Later iterations have been developed by 343 Industries.

Grand Theft Auto V: Rockstar Games' 2013 *GTA* release is a video game for the ages—a sprawling open world featuring three protagonists in and around seedy Los Santos (a fictionalized version of Los Angeles). The game was released on Xbox and PlayStation systems, along with online, a chance for users on any platform to experience a top-notch, visually stunning, endlessly intriguing video game world. The game has sold more than 120 million copies, behind only *Tetris* and *Minecraft*.[14]

Mass Effect 2: The futuristic role-playing game, which became available on Xbox in 2010, a year ahead of PlayStation 3, involves Commander Shepard leading a team on a suicide mission to save humanity. The game features complex story lines with actual consequences—your decisions and allegiances shape the final outcome. The game was praised for its heart and emphasis on diversity. *Mass Effect 2* continues to be considered among the best games of all time roughly a decade after its release.

BioShock: The 2007 masterpiece centers around Jack, whose plane crashes in the Atlantic Ocean and he ends up in the underwater city of Rapture, created as a utopia by a tycoon named Andrew Ryan. The game—a blend of first-person shooter, role-playing game, and survival horror—also features a haunting story told, in part, through audio logs.

Forza Horizon: This is car racing like you've never seen—open-world games set around a Horizon racing festival. The four games, released between 2012 and 2018, are based in Colorado, France, Italy, Australia, and the UK, and offer a wide range of marquee cars like Lamborghinis and McLarens. The open-world concept means you can drive wherever you want and complete tasks in any order. And 2018's *Forza Horizon 4* features changing seasons—from slick snow-covered winter streets and frozen lakes to thick spring puddles to give the game a fresh feel. The games are the product of Playground Games, which Microsoft acquired in 2018.

Xbox Series X

With the release of Xbox Series X—scheduled for holiday 2020—Microsoft is poised to enter a new era of gaming. The Series X will be able to play compatible Xbox games released for previous consoles—and for at least a few years, new games will be available for both of the devices. Backward compatibility means the system will release with a deep library of games.

The focus for video games goes beyond the console—it also includes other initiatives like Project xCloud, a streaming service for phones and tablets, as well as deeper Game Pass offerings. PlayStation is also gearing up to release a new console in late 2020, the PS5, that also features backward compatibility, slick graphics, and even improved energy efficiency.

But Series X, for the first time in the twenty-year console wars, shows Microsoft poised to take the lead—a reflection of determination, grit, and resolve not so dissimilar to a group of futuristic soldiers fighting aliens in a faraway land.

"Hello, I'm a Mac."

"And I'm a PC."

CHAPTER SIX

"I . . . LOVE . . . THIS . . . COMPANY!"

Steve Ballmer danced and shrieked across the stage like he'd spent the day injecting adrenaline and caffeine into his veins, a ball of energy hopscotching in an oxford and khakis. "Get up!" he yelled at the crowd, jumping halfway to the ceiling as Gloria Estefan's "Get on Your Feet" played over the loudspeakers. Ballmer's doughy body, sweat-drenched shirts, and cul-de-sac of hair were a departure from the wry geekdom of Bill Gates, who remained a giant presence in the company despite stepping down as CEO. As Ballmer stood behind the podium, he took some time to catch his breath. "I have four words for ya: I . . . Love . . . This . . . Company! Yeah!" he shouted as he pointed his fingers and clapped.[1]

Ballmer was the hype man best known for his "monkey boy dance"—the internet isn't always kind—and while Gates had a different title (chairman and chief software architect), Microsoft was still viewed as his company. He was the cofounder, after all. Gates hadn't had a boss since his high school coding days with Paul Allen. That wasn't going to change now. Gates had founded the company, and he'd brought on Ballmer in 1980, and he launched the products that defined the company's success, and he greenlighted all the initiatives in the pipeline, and he was the world's richest man, and he was still *Bill Gates*, even if he didn't have the title of CEO, and he was not going away.

Ballmer wanted to forge his own path as CEO but struggled in Gates's massive shadow. With Gates's presence looming, Ballmer couldn't fully break free, even as he jumped across the stage and sweated through his shirts. The reversed roles were difficult for Gates and Ballmer, they both later conceded. But Microsoft was much bigger than two men's egos.

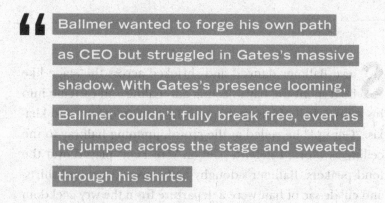

> Ballmer wanted to forge his own path as CEO but struggled in Gates's massive shadow. With Gates's presence looming, Ballmer couldn't fully break free, even as he jumped across the stage and sweated through his shirts.

As 2000 turned to 2001, with the government's case still casting a cloud over the company, Microsoft looked to the future with a new GUI, its first since Windows 95—called Windows XP—that was built off of the Windows NT kernel. Microsoft was also planning to release its first video game console, the Xbox, in late 2001.

But all of that took a back seat on a sunny Tuesday morning in September, when America was attacked by terrorists. Hijacked planes crashed into the World Trade Center towers in

New York and the Pentagon in Washington, DC, and a fourth plane went down in Shanksville, Pennsylvania. The September 11, 2001, attacks killed nearly three thousand people that day. Thousands more would die of 9/11-related illnesses in the decades that followed.

Microsoft provided tech support for the companies whose offices were destroyed in the attack, such as Cantor Fitzgerald, which inhabited the 101st to 105th floors of One World Trade Center above the first plane's impact zone and lost nearly two-thirds of its workforce. Within days of the attacks, Microsoft also announced it was releasing a software patch for its popular *Flight Simulator* computer game, in which players could fly a plane directly into the Twin Towers.

Start Another Brand-New Day

Amid the backdrop of tragedy, Microsoft in October 2001 launched Windows XP, holding its main launch event in a mourning New York City. "Today, it really is actually the end of the MS-DOS era," Gates told the audience on October 25, 2001, at the Windows XP launch party. "It's also, we would say, the end of the Windows 95 era."[2]

While Microsoft's previous Windows offerings all operated on top of that same MS-DOS operating system Microsoft had developed for the IBM PC in 1981, its new product, Windows XP, was built off of the Windows NT kernel. Gates, speaking to the crowd in Times Square, ushered in the end of the MS-DOS era by typing "exit," leading to an exchange between the Microsoft founder and an ominous computer voice reminiscent of HAL 9000 in *2001: A Space Odyssey*. At the time, MS-DOS-based Windows was running on four hundred million PCs.

Gates was joined onstage by New York City mayor Rudy Giuliani as the city still reeled following the attacks. "I thank you and all the other businesses that are here for this launch of this new product, which really couldn't come at a better time for the city of New York," Giuliani said.

As part of the XP launch, rock star Sting performed a free concert in New York's Bryant Park. "Start another brand-new day," he sang. The launch was a part of Microsoft's—and the country's—brand-new day, a chance for distraction amid sadness and strife.

XP (standing for "eXPerience") wowed users with its improved user interface, multimedia capabilities, and performance compared to the iconic Windows 95. The release, which took the place of merged, never-released Windows 2000 products for consumers and businesses, was a smash success. But it also marked the beginning of a new licensing model and product activation system that frustrated users. You couldn't install XP on numerous computers—you needed additional licenses for other computers—and installation without an internet connection was a pain.

The 9/11 attacks were so raw and crushing, and they put everything else in context—the XP launch, the antitrust case, the so-called "browser war." None of it meant quite as much anymore. Thousands of civilians were dead. America was at war with an enemy it struggled to understand, its way of life and sense of security forever changed.

The Bush administration was never all that interested in pursuing the split of Microsoft, and now it had bigger things to worry about. So, on November 2, 2001, the DOJ and Microsoft reached a settlement that barred the company from reaching exclusionary licensing agreements with PC manufacturers and requiring Microsoft to give software makers access to its source code.

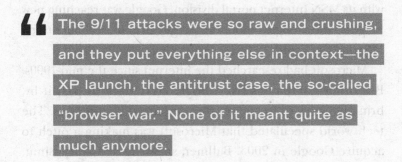

> The 9/11 attacks were so raw and crushing, and they put everything else in context—the XP launch, the antitrust case, the so-called "browser war." None of it meant quite as much anymore.

"This is a difficult time for our nation and our economy. While this settlement imposes new rules and regulations, we believe that settling the case now is the right thing to do for our customers, for the technology industry, and for the economy," Gates said.

Steve Ballmer's Appeal

Ballmer was a more affable leader than Gates. He wasn't nearly as inclined to belittle employees the way Gates had. Ballmer, secretly an introvert, was helped to get out of his shell by serving as Harvard's football manager, hyping up the team as he discussed mundane things. High energy suited him.

Gates and Ballmer had complementary skills. Where Gates was a tech wizard with a sharp business approach, Ballmer was a master salesman who appreciated his team's tech developments. But what direction would the company take under Ballmer? What would Microsoft do next? And what was Microsoft's identity?

One area that drew Ballmer's attention was search engines, specifically a start-up founded by Stanford University grad students called Google. While Microsoft struggled to break even with its MSN Internet portal division, Google was reaching new heights, and Google cofounder Sergey Brin in 2003 identified Microsoft as a rival.

Microsoft had researched the internet since the mid-1990s. But other companies like Google continued to pass it by, bringing services to market that surpassed its offerings. The tech world speculated that Microsoft was making a pitch to acquire Google in 2003. Ballmer, speaking at a symposium, fueled speculation by telling tech officials to "stand by for news" regarding an acquisition. But Google was not selling—it ended up rebuffing a takeover offer from Microsoft. Why join them when you can beat them?

Building a Legacy

What would Bill Gates do with the rest of his life beyond Microsoft? Where Microsoft's other cofounder, Paul Allen, was dipping his toe into philanthropic work, and owning sports teams such as the Portland Trailblazers and Seattle Seahawks, Gates struggled to find the focus for his second act. Simply dumping money on problems wasn't the answer.

The Bill and Melinda Gates Foundation was established in 2000—a merging of the couple's previous charitable efforts—to tackle hard problems: disease containment, providing clean drinking water, addressing waste problems in Third World countries, closing the education gap. The company also committed to finding a cure for the disease COVID-19 following a global coronavirus outbreak in early 2020.

The foundation's name speaks to the balance of power, a shared collaboration between husband and wife. Bill and

Melinda Gates looked back at the charity's first twenty years with a letter in early 2020.[3] "When we first started this work, we were optimistic about the power of innovation to drive progress—and excited about the role we could play by taking risks to unlock it," the couple wrote. "Twenty years later, we're just as optimistic—and we're still swinging for the fences. But we now have a much deeper understanding of how important it is to ensure that innovation is distributed equitably. If only some people in some places are benefitting from new advances, then others are falling even further behind."

Regulation from Across the Pond

Regulation of Microsoft didn't go away after the US government settled its case. And this time, the threat was coming from overseas—the European Commission, the EU's executive arm. The commission alleged that Microsoft had a "near monopoly" and was using Windows to dominate its rivals. The biggest issue involved Microsoft bundling Windows with its Media Player.

The case—which came about due to Sun Microsystems' complaint to the commission in 1998—resulted in Microsoft being fined a record of nearly five hundred million euros, or more than $600 million US, in 2004. Under the ruling, Microsoft was required to release a version of Windows in Europe that didn't feature a bundled Media Player.

Microsoft paid the full fine, but not before publishing a seven-page takedown of the ruling. "The Decision goes well beyond established legal precedents by asserting a broad and ill-defined duty on dominant firms to share the fruits of their research and development with other companies in the same product market," Microsoft wrote.[4] The company was subsequently slapped with more than $350 million in additional fines in 2006 for compliance failures.

The Rise of Mobile

It's easy, looking back now, to think that Microsoft didn't recognize the potential of smartphones, that it was somehow unaware of the industry's direction. But that wasn't quite accurate. Microsoft released its first smartphone, the Windows CE, in 1996, and foresaw the rise of streaming video services and tablet devices.

In 1999, Microsoft developed its view of a connected future—one featuring touch computing, video chat, voice commands, and smart TVs. Those futuristic perspectives appeared in a concept video, called "Meet the Family," that Microsoft aired at CES.

The company simply struggled to recognize how to monetize the potential of the mobile world or came to market with its products at the wrong time, a malaise that settled over the company under Ballmer. When you have more than fifty thousand employees and a market cap of $300 billion, it's difficult to recognize the right time to shift, to abandon the central strengths that have been successful to your company in favor of something new.

Microsoft wasn't nimble—it was beginning to resemble the companies it had bested a generation earlier like Lotus and IBM. Under its two masters, Ballmer and Gates, Microsoft struggled to make up its mind and get its timing right.

Zune

Microsoft had gotten used to entering markets dominated by others and building off of their efforts—creating a "better" operating system or GUI or internet browser. The Zune served a similar purpose. Microsoft introduced the Zune in 2006 as a rival to Apple's breakout iPod music player, which had been introduced in 2001. Zune was exciting—it featured a bigger screen and longer battery life than the iPod, and quickly became the No. 2 portable music player.

Microsoft finally had an answer to the iPod. But months after the Zune was released, Apple unveiled its newest gadget—the iPhone. The iPhone could allow you to make calls and answer emails and listen to music, all on the same device. The iPhone was disruptive. And stellar. A user could scroll across the screen with their finger, and the interface consisted of a screen and "home" button—no clunky keyboard, meaning more screen space and smarter usability for apps.

With the iPhone and other competing devices coming to market, no one had much use for a Zune.

The iPhone caused Google to adjust its strategy for its mysterious Android mobile project, which had been in development for about two years. "As a consumer I was blown away. I wanted one immediately. But as a Google engineer, I thought 'We're going to have to start over,'" Google engineer Chris DeSalvo told the *Atlantic*. "What we had suddenly looked just so . . . nineties. It's just one of those things that are obvious when you see it."[5]

But that reality wasn't obvious for Ballmer and Microsoft, which doubled down on what previously worked. Early Windows Mobile devices—and phones by other manufacturers that ran Microsoft operating systems—were standard models that featured a built-in keyboard or used a stylus. The screens were smaller and less dynamic and didn't use touch screen. The year before the iPhone launch, 2006, Microsoft's Windows Mobile operating system held a 56 percent market share for personal digital assistants in 2006, and ten million devices running Windows Mobile were shipped. Ballmer, when asked about the iPhone on CNBC in 2007, laughed.[6]

"Five hundred dollars? Fully subsidized? With a plan? I said, 'That is the most expensive phone in the world.' And it doesn't appeal to business customers because it doesn't have a keyboard, which makes it not a very good email machine. It may sell very well," Ballmer added. "We have our strategy; we've got great Windows Mobile devices in the market today. You can get a Motorola Q phone now for $99; it's a very capable machine. It'll do music, it'll do internet, it'll do email, it'll do instant messaging, so I kind of look at that and I say, 'Well, I like our strategy. I like it a lot.'"[7]

Even though Apple was the first to market with its new technology, built on an iOS operating system, Apple would only make up about 20 percent of the mobile phone market. It was the old PC vs. Mac debate all over again, in phone form. Microsoft often won, and it expected to win this time, too. And then it didn't.

Android

Ballmer wasn't only laughing at the iPhone, he also had a habit of chuckling about Google's mobile phone project whenever asked about it, pointing out (accurately) that Google hadn't sold a single phone the year before. The giggles reflected Ballmer's inner optimism, his desire to convey confidence in the face of the unknown, a poker player trying to bluff with a middling hand. Instead of folding on Microsoft's mobile phone strategy, Ballmer raised.

But Google's Android project, released in 2008, was no laughing matter for Microsoft. Android reached the marketplace after Apple's iOS but was equally disruptive. Google made the smart decision to encourage third-party developers with an open-source operating system. Google also bundled all of the apps a user would need—its Gmail, maps, calendar, and instant messaging offerings. Meanwhile, Microsoft took until 2010 to release Windows Phone, which was built on its Windows CE platform.

"The industry moved forward faster than we could catch up," Terry Myerson, who guided the Windows Mobile team, admitted years later in a LinkedIn post.[8]

Microsoft charged third-party developers, incentivizing them further to work with Android and Apple. Microsoft left an opening and didn't recognize the changing needs of the marketplace, and Google capitalized, building a special team around its Android acquisition to solve the mobile problem, and driving Android to become the standard of the non-iPhone world.

Microsoft tried to claw back. Along the way, it released and pulled back a phone line—the Kin One and Kin Two—through Verizon in early 2010 that featured slide-out keyboards but no additional apps for download and no GPS, unsophisticated phones in a smartphone era. Advertisements for the Kin showed a group of college-aged users taking photos of their bodies (um . . .) and sending the photos to each other. The Kin was also shown on the CW's *Gossip Girl* as a way to draw in teen users. Kin was initially slated for international launch, but after sluggish sales, it was restricted to the US only, and then it disappeared.

Later that year, Microsoft released the Windows Phone 7 operating system, and Windows Phone 8 followed in 2012—last gasps at chewing away Android's market advantage. But with a lack of apps compared to Android (Windows Phone was missing YouTube and Instagram), and without solid native apps like Gmail,[9] the outcome was all but final. Microsoft tried to hedge its bets by partnering with, and later purchasing, smartphone maker Nokia. The $7.2 billion deal was finalized in 2013. But by then, Android had won.

Ballmer and Gates both consider the rise of mobile among their biggest missed opportunities. Microsoft was still successful by any measurement—one of the world's most influential and valuable companies. But it was missing something. The magic was gone. The PC king struggled in the mobile age.

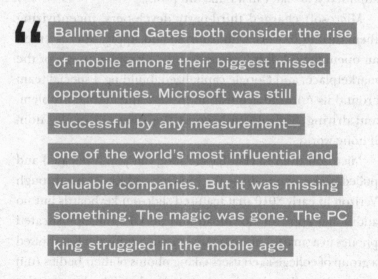

Ballmer and Gates both consider the rise of mobile among their biggest missed opportunities. Microsoft was still successful by any measurement—one of the world's most influential and valuable companies. But it was missing something. The magic was gone. The PC king struggled in the mobile age.

Vista

The video opens to show the world's saddest party, featuring two men addressing the camera and four people behind them.

"Hello, I'm a Mac," hip, jeans-wearing actor Justin Long says.

"And I'm a PC," his stuffy, suited counterpart (humorist John Hodgman) responds.

"Well, after five years, Vista's finally here," Long says.

"Whoopee for the whole entire world," Hodgman says, twirling his finger.[10]

"What's wrong?"

"What isn't wrong? I mean, my new operating system arrives, I've had nothing but problems. I had to buy a new graphics card, get new memory, now I can't even use some of my software and peripherals. I mean, let's face it . . . this party's a bust."

The commercial—one of dozens of Apple's "Get a Mac" ads—was Apple at its most savage, skewering Microsoft's long-awaited operating system. Windows Vista, which was first conceived under codename "Longhorn" in 2001, faced numerous stops and starts and shifts on its way to the marketplace in late 2006 and early 2007. The biggest focus was stronger security than its predecessor, Windows XP, which featured vulnerabilities that made it susceptible to malware and viruses. But Vista was derided for its extensive system requirements, and it also included long-term licensing agreements that locked in a license to a specific device.

While sales for Vista were initially soft, the operating system went on to attract four hundred million users. But Ballmer, reflecting on his tenure as CEO in an interview with Bloomberg, admitted that Vista was one of the factors taking attention away from Microsoft's mobile efforts.

"We should have been in the hardware business sooner in the phone case, and we were still suffering what I would call some of the effects of our Vista release of Windows, which sucked up a huge amount of resource for a much longer period of time than it should have because we stumbled over it. And when you have a lot of your best engineers sort of in a sense, being nonproductive for a while, it really takes a toll," Ballmer said.[11]

During the same time period of Vista, Microsoft also made a $6 billion acquisition of aQuantive Inc., a digital marketing and advertising firm, in 2007 as a way to keep pace with Yahoo and Google, which had purchased the digital marketing company DoubleClick. While the acquisition of aQuantive itself was not a bad one, the price left analysts "totally shocked," fueling speculation that Microsoft was getting desperate.

The Long Goodbye

Microsoft was Bill Gates. Bill Gates was Microsoft. But by 2006, the company's cofounder was ready to begin the long goodbye as an employee. He would depart Microsoft in 2008, joining the company board but having no day-to-day role. Gates had built the company from the desert in New Mexico, from those days when his secretary would find him passed out on the ground from working so many hours.

You have to be talented to survive so many years in the ever-evolving tech world—but the job required more than talent. You needed vision and business sense and the ability to evolve and to build the right team and keep investors happy and weather the storms and put out a high percentage of hit products and minimize the mistakes.

By the time Gates departed Microsoft, many of his closest contemporaries were long gone, and even those that were still around—such as Apple's Steve Jobs—had taken detours. Jobs departed Apple in 1987 and was gone from the company for nearly a decade before returning.

What else did Gates have to accomplish at Microsoft? For all that he'd done, he had bigger things to do through the Bill and Melinda Gates Foundation. Gates was going to change the world, again.

Spoofs and Goofs

While Gates and Ballmer drifted apart as friends, they relished making videos together that spoofed popular movies. Many of the videos were played for audiences at trade shows and other events. In one, Gates plays the comedic spy Austin Powers while Ballmer plays the bald Dr. Evil (he had the hair, or lack of it, to pull off the part). Another saw them playing dim-witted clubgoers from *Night at the Roxbury*. There was also a spoof of *The Matrix*, with Ballmer playing Keanu Reeves's Neo role and Gates as the guru Morpheus. The most nostalgic video shows Ballmer and Gates on a playdate—riding a two-person bicycle, playing bumper cars, swinging at the park, fishing, and participating in a game of catch.

Bing

Microsoft had struggled in search. Google was the industry leader. Live Search and MSN Search failed to make an impact. After Microsoft tried, and failed, to buy Yahoo for $47.5 billion in 2008, the company decided to launch a new search service: Bing. The search engine, previously known as "Kumo," had some interesting features, such as the ability to preview websites by hovering over links. But more than a Google competitor, Bing offered a chance for the company to embrace technologies it had overlooked or failed to capture, such as global cloud-first services. Amazon, the e-commerce company, had launched its cloud computing platform, Amazon Web Services, or AWS, in 2006.

Bing helped Microsoft weave an "intelligent fabric" across its platforms, a tech infrastructure index driving advancement.[12] Important figures guided Microsoft's progress. Dr. Qi Lu, previously an executive at Yahoo, was hired as head of all online services. Another key move involved Satya Nadella, a Microsoft employee since 1992 who Ballmer promoted to run the company's online search and advertising business, tackling issues involving cloud infrastructure. The promotion came with a warning. "This might be your last job at Microsoft," Ballmer told Nadella, "because if you fail there is no parachute. You may just crash with it."[13]

Under Nadella's guidance, Bing succeeded in indirect but significant ways. It wasn't going to change Google's market dominance. Microsoft also didn't need that. "The search engine that many had said should be shuttered in its early days of struggle . . . today is a profitable multibillion-dollar business for Microsoft. Just as important, though, was how it helped to jump-start our move to the cloud," Nadella wrote in his book, *Hit Refresh*.

In time, Satya Nadella was tasked with leading Microsoft's server and tools business—an area that had been plagued by corporate mistrust, infighting, and a lack of direction. An internal struggle persisted about the cloud, holding Microsoft back from innovation. It wasn't making money and the employees weren't unified and some of them were bitter that Nadella was promoted instead of them.

"I had to convince my team to adapt a counterintuitive strategy—to shift focus from the big server and tools business that paid everyone's salary to the tiny cloud business with almost no revenue," Nadella recalled. So Nadella charted a course. The servers allowed Microsoft to provide a hybrid cloud service, a mix of private and public cloud. Under Nadella's watch, a side project that had the code name Red Dog started taking shape—it would eventually go by the name Azure.

A global network of giant data processing centers, Azure offers the infrastructure and storage for companies to carry out their computing needs. The development of Azure allowed Microsoft to deepen its offerings.

Office 365—a suite of cloud-based business services—was launched in June 2011, giving subscribers a chance to use web apps, along with the web-based document and storage platform SharePoint, Exchange email, and Lync, instant messaging software that preceded the company's acquisition of Skype. Slowly but surely, Amazon's AWS finally had competition.

Surface

Ballmer's vision for the company involved a new look at hardware, something the company had largely avoided. Microsoft historically found its biggest success with software. But the Xbox proved that the company could succeed in developing devices (the "Red Ring of Death" issue notwithstanding).

Ballmer wanted to push deeper into hardware. Gates, now the most influential member of the company's board, didn't agree. There was good reason for skepticism. Products like the Zune music player failed to make the right impact, and the risk of failure with hardware was greater—developing software was expensive in man hours but didn't come with the same materials cost. Hardware needed to have a long shelf life and last through numerous patches and software updates.

Following its pattern to wait, and wait, and wait some more before entering a new market, Microsoft slowly developed a tablet. Apple had its iPad, Google and Asus had the Nexus 7, and Microsoft was ready to release the Surface. The new division—representing the company's first PC—was announced in June 2012 and released that October.

The device, a pairing of Microsoft's hardware and software, featured some neat touches. The magnetic cover turned into a full multitouch keyboard, and apps appeared on the screen in a tiled format. The Surface was not a breakout hit—sales lagged, and Ballmer later admitted that Microsoft lost $900 million. Much like the Xbox, the release set a path for Microsoft's future, a direction for further opportunity. By the time the Surface Pro 3 was released in 2014 with its x64 Intel CPU and Windows 8 operating system, Microsoft was finally making a dent in the mobile devices market.

> By the time the Surface Pro 3 was released in 2014 with its x64 Intel CPU and Windows 8 operating system, Microsoft was finally making a dent in the mobile devices market.

Outlook.com

The email product Outlook.com debuted in 2013, giving Microsoft a better chance to compete with Google's popular Gmail. Microsoft's previous email service, Hotmail, was acquired in 1997 but was surpassed by Yahoo! Mail and Google's Gmail.

Outlook—which drew more than sixty million users during its preview—was especially popular for companies given its use of the file hosting service OneDrive to allow for sharing huge files. After shifting its Hotmail users to Outlook, Microsoft's email platform had four hundred million users, a close competitor to Gmail.

The Turnaround

The turnaround was in the works. After some shaky results, Ballmer had begun righting the ship. But in August 2013, facing pressure from the Bill Gates–led board of directors, Ballmer announced he was going to step aside as CEO.

"I love this company," he wrote in a retirement letter, echoing his words on the stage in 2001, when he danced like his veins were full of caffeine and adrenaline. "I love the way we helped invent and popularize computing and the PC. I love the bigness and boldness of our bets. I love our people and their talent and our willingness to accept and embrace their range of capabilities, including their quirks. I love the way we embrace and work with other companies to change the world and succeed together. I love the breadth and diversity of our customers, from consumer to enterprise, across industries, countries, and people of all backgrounds and age groups."

While Ballmer's time as CEO didn't provide enough short-term, clear-cut victories, and the company failed to properly capitalize on mobile, he sowed the seeds for the company's regrowth, shifting focus to cloud computing with Azure and unveiling lines that would establish Microsoft as a hardware company in addition to a software company—Xbox and Surface. He also endured the long shadow of Bill Gates, the aftershocks of antitrust cases on two continents, the bursting dot-com bubble, a terror attack that hobbled the economy, and the worst economic recession since the stock market crash of 1929. Not an easy stretch for any business leader.

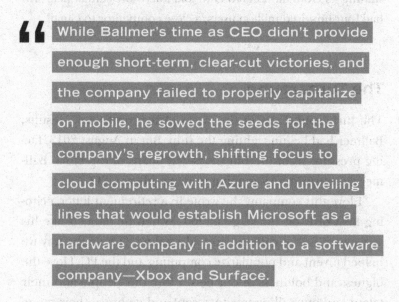

" While Ballmer's time as CEO didn't provide enough short-term, clear-cut victories, and the company failed to properly capitalize on mobile, he sowed the seeds for the company's regrowth, shifting focus to cloud computing with Azure and unveiling lines that would establish Microsoft as a hardware company in addition to a software company—Xbox and Surface.

Indecision and missed opportunities allowed other companies—namely Apple, Google, Amazon, and Facebook—to jump ahead of Microsoft in mobile, search, cloud, and social media. Even so, Employee No. 30 departed with Microsoft's market cap at about $250 billion.

"Steve was intensely emotional, and that emotion was true and real," recalls former Microsoft communications employee

Mario Juarez. "And when he cared, he was 100 pecent. There was not much of a dial. He was just intense. And I think he deeply loved the company and I think he deeply loved what he was doing. He was a really good guy, a super-smart guy who, maybe he had some blind spots, but I don't think he gets the credit for being the caretaker of the company that he was. He was an amazing administrator and motivator, and he could be immense fun to be with."[14]

The company embarked on an extensive search to find Ballmer's replacement. It was assumed Microsoft would look externally for the next CEO, to bring in someone fresh and new to change the company's culture. But maybe that wasn't necessary. Maybe there was someone already within Microsoft who was ready to guide the tech giant to new heights.

What's in a (Code)Name?

Microsoft has made a habit of using special codewords to identify its marquee products still under development—a habit that draws intrigue and speculation about the company's plans. Here are some of the most notable codenames used throughout Microsoft's history.

- Chicago: Project that would become Windows 95
- O'Hare: Internet Explorer
- Cairo: Long-gestating 1990s Windows project that was eventually canceled
- Sparta, Winball: Windows 3.1 Plus
- Utopia: Bob (note: this product was not utopia by any stretch)
- Thunder: Visual Basic 1.0

- Longhorn: Windows Vista
- Red Dog: Azure
- Project Scarlett: Xbox Series X
- Ozone: Windows Mobile 2003
- Blue: Windows 9.1
- Threshold: Windows 10 RTM and 1511

"It's not about our technology, it's about what other people can do with our technology."

—SATYA NADELLA,
CEO of Microsoft

CHAPTER SEVEN

A NEW ERA

Satya Nadella stood beside Bill Gates and Steve Ballmer as hundreds of Microsoft employees swarmed around the stage. "This company's had three CEOs. They're all right here," Gates said during the February 5, 2014, event, smiling. He wore a sweater over a button-down shirt, looking grandfatherly.[1]

Ballmer, meanwhile, tucked his hands into his pants pockets as he soaked in the moment. There was no jumping, no rallying, no caffeine- and adrenaline-fueled hoots and hollers. He wasn't the center of attention—his successor was.

"This business of ours is an exciting business. And one of the core things we've gotta realize is that this business doesn't really respect tradition. What it respects is innovation on a go-forward basis," Nadella told the audience. "So it's really our collective challenge that we now need to make Microsoft thrive in a mobile-first and a cloud-first world."[2]

Nadella wasn't talking about Windows or PCs or Word or Excel. He saw two overlooked technologies—mobile and cloud—

as Microsoft's vehicle to sustained success. In his first day as CEO, the forty-six-year-old Nadella provided a road map for everyone in the company. He reinforced that vision in an interview secretly recorded days earlier featuring Nadella and Microsoft Chief Storyteller Steve Clayton doing a short walk-and-talk interview through a building on Microsoft's campus.

"We did one take on it and we were both really happy with it. The team said, 'Hey, let's just do one more take just to give it another run,'" Clayton said. The interviewer asked Nadella five questions. Nadella suggested one of his first jobs as CEO was to "ruthlessly remove any obstacles that allow us to innovate."

"That line just really stuck with me," Clayton said.

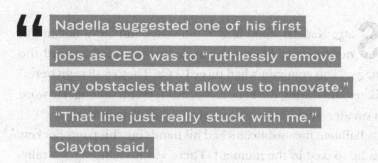

Nadella suggested one of his first jobs as CEO was to "ruthlessly remove any obstacles that allow us to innovate." "That line just really stuck with me," Clayton said.

Nadella got to work updating the company's mission statement, too. Microsoft had grown significantly from the days of a computer on every desk running Microsoft products. The new goal: "to empower every person and every organization on the planet to achieve more."

Innovation over Bureaucracy

Nadella had risen through the ranks since joining the company in 1992—first on the Windows NT team, and later an executive for the Online Services Division before serving as president of the Server & Tools Division. He "wanted to work for a company filled with people who believed they were on a mission to change the world," he wrote in his 2017 book, *Hit Refresh*.[3]

He got to work fixing the bureaucracy, internal politics, and infighting that had plagued the company. He wanted to remove the barriers blocking innovation. So he swapped a staid employee meeting with One Week, a series of events "designed to inform employees about, and inspire them to engage in, the company's vision and strategy," the *Seattle Times* reported.[4]

The centerpiece of One Week was a hackathon—a chance for thousands of employees to pitch and collaborate on special projects. The projects ranged from technology for people in wheelchairs to addressing sexism in video games.[5] The initiative gave employees a chance to work across departments as they found creative ways to solve problems. Some of the projects were eventually developed for wider release—new business opportunities borne from collaboration.

A Different Kind of Leader

One of Nadella's strengths is his preternatural calm—he's not known to belittle employees, a la Bill Gates, or jump and yell like Steve Ballmer. He exudes a collected air, unflappable cool. He's prepared and seasoned. No ego. No pretense. No drama. And no arrogance about decades of success, either. "At Microsoft we have this very bad habit of not being able to push ourselves because we just feel very self-satisfied with the success we've had," he told Bloomberg in 2019. "We're learning how not to look at the past."[6]

A big part of Nadella's strategy boils down to one phrase: "growth mindset." The mentality is at the center of Dr. Carol Dweck's book *Mindset: The New Psychology of Success,* which considers how we limit or bolster our opportunities based on the mindset we embrace. A growth mindset means continuing to learn and build and climb. Nadella stressed the importance of a growth mindset for Microsoft staffers. Any change at Microsoft would come from within its employees.

Mario Juarez, a longtime former Microsoft employee who worked with all three of the company's CEOs, says he was captivated by Nadella's nature, saying he was "different" from other tech leaders. "He was really nice to people. He went out of his way to care about how people were and what their experience was. And he was gentle. Super, super smart guy. And not a pushover at all, but he projects this image of this magnanimous, thoughtful, soulful guy, which is definitely a part of who he is," Juarez said.[7]

Hard Decisions

Nadella's first product unveiling as CEO spoke to his aims and collaborative approach—Office software for Apple's iPad. "This is our first step on the journey of making this great innovation vector for all of Microsoft," he said.

Nadella wasn't worried about chasing every carrot and going after the hot product—that's how Microsoft failed with Zune and other devices. It got distracted by what every other company was doing and missed the bigger picture. Nadella was focused on the bigger picture, and he needed to make some difficult decisions as he took the company in a different direction than his predecessor. In July 2014, Microsoft laid off 18,000 employees—about 14 pecent of its workforce, and the biggest layoffs in the company's history. Most of the employees had been part of the Nokia acquisition.

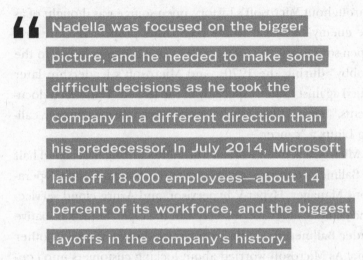

> Nadella was focused on the bigger picture, and he needed to make some difficult decisions as he took the company in a different direction than his predecessor. In July 2014, Microsoft laid off 18,000 employees—about 14 percent of its workforce, and the biggest layoffs in the company's history.

Nadella, in an email to employees, stressed that the changes would keep the company agile. The layoffs also marked a departure from hardware and a pivot away from projects like low-priced Nokia Asha phones, as well as Nokia X phones that used the Android platform. Additional layoffs were announced in July 2015 and May 2016.

The hard choices were necessary in order for Microsoft to refocus. What the company was doing wasn't working anymore. And underperforming Nokia phones weren't going to change those problems. Microsoft wasn't going to win with its own phones—not yet, anyway. It needed to get its apps and programs running on as many devices as possible, regardless of the brand name and operating system, and stop trying to fight a losing battle.

"Open" for Business

Throughout Microsoft's history, open-source was thought of as the enemy—a threat to the company's proprietary software. Open-source was the focus of Bill Gates's "Open Letter to the Hobby" during the 1970s, and Microsoft's leadership later railed against Linux, especially in the leaked "Halloween documents." Steve Ballmer took the criticisms one step further, calling Linux a "cancer."

Microsoft actually worked with Linux during the second half of Ballmer's tenure—including with its System Center Operations Manager, Hyper-V hypervisor, and Azure cloud service. The company had also worked with the Open Source Initiative under Ballmer. But it had also resisted open-source in other ways. As Microsoft worried about locking customers into contracts to use its software and apps, developers embraced an open-source world that encouraged users to work with and modify code—a collaborative process that allowed for the development of an improved product.

The power of open-source is visible in Google's popular mobile operating system, Android, which is made up of elements available under open-source licenses. Working with open-source encouraged developers—and resulted in better products and services. Open-source also helped drive the success of Microsoft rivals such as Google and Amazon. Instead of trying to swim against the open-source current, Microsoft could swim with it—and become a friend, and not a foe, to developers.

Nadella was a driving force in that culture shift, and his mindset was aided by other open-source advocates joining the company. Open-source was a bigger threat when being avoided than embraced. The actual cancer wasn't Linux, per se; it was Microsoft's holier-than-thou self-exclusion that kept the company from fully embracing its role as industry leader.

"Dogma at Microsoft had long held that the open-source software from Linux was the enemy. We couldn't afford to cling to that attitude any longer. We had to meet the customers where they were and, more importantly, we needed to ensure that we viewed our opportunity not through a rearview mirror, but with a more future-oriented perspective," he wrote in *Hit Refresh*.[8]

Microsoft ♥ Linux?

Microsoft showed its commitment to open-source with initiatives that would have been seen as heretical a generation prior. Azure—Nadella's previous department—best represented Microsoft's new approach. Lots of Azure's code is made up of Linux, and Microsoft began offering open-source databases on Azure. To reflect the changing mindset, Windows Azure was renamed Microsoft Azure.

"Our commitment to deliver an enterprise-grade cloud platform for the world's applications is greater than ever," Microsoft Azure GM Steven Martin said in a statement announcing the name change. "Today we support one of the broadest set of operating systems, languages, and services of any public cloud—from Windows, SQL and .NET to Python, Ruby, Node.js, Java, Hadoop, Linux, and Oracle. In today's mobile-first, cloud-first, data-powered world, customers want a public cloud

platform that supports their needs—whatever they may be—
and that public cloud is Microsoft Azure."[9]

The same Microsoft that once tried to rule the internet was
letting customers know it would support their needs *whatever
they may be.* No, Microsoft wasn't open-sourcing its keystone
products, but this was different. Company leaders like Scott
Hanselman, Rajesh Jha, Scott Guthrie, and Harry Shum were
tasked with upholding Microsoft's open-source efforts. Without
buy-in from key figures, Nadella's goals would fall flat.

Hanselman highlighted the generational stigma surround-
ing Microsoft in a 2014 blog post, "Microsoft killed my Pappy."[10]

"I think that Microsoft is very aware of perceptions and is
actively trying to counter them by *actually being open*," he wrote.
"I'd say we're more concerned than a Google or Apple about
how folks perceive us." There was also the 2014 announcement[11]
that the .NET Core software framework would be open-source,
with a cross-platform foundation and stronger ecosystem.

"If you think about it: open-source is essentially the ultimate
agile development style. Every change is immediately public
and (in theory) consumable," Immo Landwerth, Program
Manager for .NET, wrote.

Microsoft also launched an open-source website[12] devoted to
projects—including Visual Studio Code, TypeScript, and .NET.
"Whether you're a seasoned open source developer or looking
to make your first ever open source contribution Microsoft has
many open source projects seeking new contributors. All issues
below need your help!"

The messaging was reinforced by Nadella. During a press
and analyst briefing in 2015, he appeared before a slide:
"Microsoft ♥ Linux."

A company blog hammered the point home: "You run workloads on Windows. You run workloads on Linux. You run these

workloads in your on-premises datacenters, hosted at service providers, and in public clouds. You just want it all to work, and to work together regardless of the operating system. We hear you, and understand that your world is heterogeneous. Bottom line, this is a business opportunity for Microsoft to offer heterogeneous support—both Windows and Linux workloads—on-premises and in a public cloud. Microsoft can add real value in a heterogeneous cloud."[13]

Other collaborations reinforced Microsoft's embrace of open-source. In 2016, the company joined the Linux Foundation, an organization that "supports the creation of sustainable open source ecosystems by providing financial and intellectual resources, infrastructure, services, events, and training."[14] One of the foundation's board members is Sarah Novotny, a longtime open-source champion and part of the Microsoft Azure Office of the CTO. The following year, Microsoft became a premium sponsor of the Open Source Initiative, a corporation devoted to the usage of open-source software.

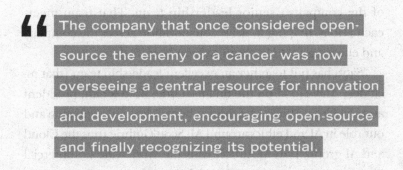

The company that once considered open-source the enemy or a cancer was now overseeing a central resource for innovation and development, encouraging open-source and finally recognizing its potential.

Microsoft has been partnering with Red Hat, an open-source company, since 2015 to bring Red Hat Enterprise Linux to Azure. And Microsoft bought Github, a repository for open-source projects, in 2018 for $7.5 billion. The company that once considered open-source the enemy or a cancer was now over-seeing a central resource for innovation and development, en-couraging open-source and finally recognizing its potential.

Taking the "Lead"

As executive vice president and chief financial officer, Amy Hood is one of Microsoft's most visible leaders and among the highest-ranking female executives in the company's history. Hood—who joined Microsoft in 2002 after working at Goldman Sachs—served as CFO of Microsoft's Business Division, helping to guide the transition to Office 365 before being promoted to CFO. The Kentucky native was also involved in some of the company's key acquisitions and, beyond shifting resources to growth areas, has also made inclusion a priority. Through Nadella's urging and deep thought, she uncovered her purpose as CFO: "To help make Microsoft the most successful place it can be."[15]

Nadella considers Hood "our conscience"[16]—a key member of the company's senior leadership team. That team meets each Friday, helping to drive collaboration across the company and ensuring that Microsoft's vision is unified.

"Satya has put together an excellent leadership team [that in-cludes] Amy Hood on the financial side; Brad Smith, president and chief legal officer who thinks about policy and regulation and our role in AI and ethics around AI; Scott Guthrie runs the Cloud and AI group; Judson Althoff runs the Worldwide Commercial Business . . . it's an extremely well-balanced team, a diverse team that brings multiple experience from both inside and outside of the company," said Microsoft Chief Storyteller Steve Clayton.[17]

"The entire senior leadership team gets together every Fri-day for at least six hours. They operate incredibly well as a team, they make decisions as a team, and that rigor and discipline to meet every Friday and take six hours out of their important schedules has led to a group that is really a classic case of the sum being greater than the individual parts."

In the Clouds

Cloud computing conjures the idea of a fluffy floating mass of water drops, ready to rain on those below, but clouds like Azure or Amazon's AWS don't float—they represent a wide range of computing services. Cloud technology allows companies and governments to carry out their computing needs without buying hardware and software and setting up its own data centers.

Cloud—not Windows—was the biggest driver of Microsoft's future. Nadella cemented that focus in March 2018 by announcing a reorganization: a new Experiences & Devices team led by Rajesh Jha, and a Cloud + AI Platform overseen by Scott Guthrie. Amid the reorganization, Windows and Devices department leader Terry Myerson moved on from the company.

Jha's team was tasked with an important purpose: "to instill a unifying product ethos across our end-user experiences and devices." The reorganization—and deemphasis of Windows—came with the formation of a committee to tackle ethical issues due to AI advances. No, Windows was not going away. Windows 10 remained the dominant operating system[18] on PCs in 2020. But Windows was not the company's marquee focus anymore.

There were smart financial reasons for shifting more energy behind the cloud. For the first half of the 2020 fiscal year, Microsoft brought in $24.1 billion for its commercial cloud revenue[19]—cementing Azure as the second-ranked cloud company behind Amazon's AWS, which had a substantial head start.

Nadella saw Azure holding a significant purpose: becoming "the world's computer."

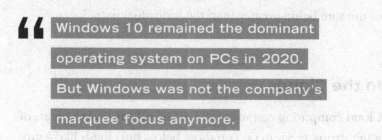

> Windows 10 remained the dominant operating system on PCs in 2020. But Windows was not the company's marquee focus anymore.

Azure by the Numbers

Azure's strength is in its network. Azure uses more than one hundred data centers—giant buildings filled with millions of servers[20]—located in places like Sao Paulo and Marseille, Canberra and Doha.

The service is available in 140 countries, and 95 percent of Fortune 500 companies use Azure.

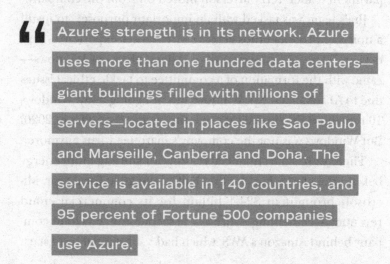

> Azure's strength is in its network. Azure uses more than one hundred data centers—giant buildings filled with millions of servers—located in places like Sao Paulo and Marseille, Canberra and Doha. The service is available in 140 countries, and 95 percent of Fortune 500 companies use Azure.

By 2020, more than four thousand companies were using Microsoft Azure, including:

- The Kindai University Aquaculture Research Institute and Toyota Tsusho Corporation collaborated with Microsoft Japan to improve and streamline its system of selecting fingerlings, young fish that have developed scales and working fins. The improvements include an automated process to regulate pump flow—easing the reliance on guesswork from workers.
- Cincinnati Children's Hospital Medical Center developed a mobile app using Microsoft Azure and Azure services that aids families—offering hospital navigation, answers to questions they may have, and entertainment for children.
- Pizza Hut Hong Kong used Azure for its server and database services and launched a new mobile app, allowing for scalability and the opportunity to engage more dynamically with customers.
- Renault Sport Formula One Team uses Microsoft Dynamics 365 for Operations, analyzing data from more than two hundred sensors in each car and using that information to pursue competitive advantages and providing input for modifications.
- Azure runs the safety operations for Chevron Corp., analyzing hundreds of terabytes of data from as many as 2,700 wells, while Microsoft's augmented-reality HoloLens headset allows engineers at Chevron offices in Houston to virtually repair equipment located in the Permian Basin. Collected data is used to optimize drilling efficiencies, but the ultimate purpose is to prevent any Deepwater Horizon-scale disasters.

Azure's power tied into Nadella's vision for the company: "We don't want to be the cool company in the tech sector. We want to be the company that makes other people cool," he wrote in *Hit Refresh*. It was a departure from the days of Steve Ballmer, when Microsoft tried to be *cool*, chasing fads and flashy gizmos (such as the ill-fated Zune).

As Nadella became established as CEO, he also brought a new approach to Bill Gates's long-standing mission, "A computer on every desk, and in every home, running Microsoft software." That mission was established during Microsoft's PC days. Microsoft won those PC days, but there were other missions ahead that had nothing to do with physical computers. Nadella helped Microsoft develop a new mission statement and a new path forward: "to empower every person and every organization on the planet to achieve more."

Paul and Bill

Microsoft's founders faced a long, strange, extremely successful journey together. It began in Lakeside's computer room and took them all the way to the top of the tech world, from BASIC to billionaires. Bill Gates and Paul Allen went through peaks and valleys in their friendship. That's bound to happen over the course of nearly half a century.

Even through the times when they weren't on close speaking terms, their mutual admiration could never be debated. That brotherly bond resonated when Allen died in 2018 after his third bout with cancer. He was sixty-five.

Gates reflected glowingly as he discussed Allen at the Forbes Philanthropy Summit in 2019. "I wish Paul had gotten to see all of the good his generosity will do," Gates told the audience.

"He was one of the most thoughtful, brilliant, and curious people I've ever met. He deserved so much more time than he got—although no one can say his wasn't a life well-lived."[21]

Changing Competition

Microsoft's history and evolving focuses are reflected in the company's competitors.

Quartz analyzed thirty years of Microsoft's annual corporate filings, stretching from 1989 to 2018, an exercise that shows how far Microsoft has come.[22] Early competitors included Lotus, Sun Microsystems, and Novell. Recent competitors include Amazon, Google, Salesforce, and Sony.

Three companies were mentioned more than any others: IBM, Apple, and Oracle.

Partnerships

Under Satya Nadella, Microsoft looked to its rivals for strategic partnerships—finding opportunity where it had previously took an isolationist approach. Microsoft made sure Office was available on Google's Android platform and Apple's iPhones, and its apps paired with Facebook, while Amazon ran Bing search on its Fire tablets.

"Partnerships like these can exist, at times uneasily, with competitors in specific product or service categories. We compete vigorously with Amazon in the cloud market; there's no ambiguity about that. But why can't Microsoft and Amazon partner in other areas? For example, Bing powers the search experience on Amazon Fire tablets."[23]

Partnership as a way to innovation—it was the same lesson Microsoft learned under Bill Gates during the 1980s, when the company grew into a superpower in large part because of its alliances with IBM and Apple. Even Microsoft's competition with Google has become friendlier—in 2016, the rivals announced they would drop regulatory complaints about each other. "Our companies compete vigorously, but we want to do so on the merits of our products, not in legal proceedings," the companies said.[24]

Nadella's message about uneasy partnerships was reinforced by Microsoft's plans for two foldable mobile devices set for release in 2020, the Surface Neo Tablet and Surface Duo phone. The devices feature dual screens that open like a book and can be adapted in numerous ways. And they run Google's Android (gasp!) operating system. After failing to stop Android and following the Nokia debacle, Microsoft was ready for another shot with mobile devices, and in the process further blurring the line between desktop and mobile.

The Next Decade

Under Nadella, the company prepared to continue driving innovation and building on its cloud growth into the 2020s. Microsoft was poised to apply and unlock the power behind its technology and data in new ways. The HoloLens 2, Microsoft's latest mixed-reality headset, was released in November 2019, covering a diagonal field of view of 52 degrees (the original had 34) and featuring improved gesture controls. HoloLens 2 presents new opportunities for businesses, especially those focused on repair work—a hands-free way to study the root cause of a problem and interact with others while simultaneously analyzing data.

With Dynamics 365, Microsoft gives businesses opportunities to transform using the strength of its cloud platform, AI, and other offerings. Releases scheduled for 2020 include "hundreds of new features," covering marketing, sales, service, finance and operations, human resources, commerce, and industry platforms.

Back on Top

Microsoft's stock price paralleled its rejuvenation. When Nadella became CEO, shares were selling in the $37 range—that value rose to $43 within his first year. Despite some peaks and valleys, the price rose significantly between 2016 and early 2020—climbing from $50 to $70 to $100 to $125 to $180, tripling in price over the course of four years. In 2018, for the first time since 2002, the company had the top market cap.

Microsoft's market cap in early 2020 was $1.4 trillion—neck and neck with Apple. But the stock price alone wasn't Nadella's end goal. He was interested in uncovering something deeper, trying to answer a fundamental question: *Why does Microsoft exist?*

The question got to the heart of Satya Nadella's aim as CEO. That search took Nadella back to the company's beginnings—past cloud and mobile devices and the Xbox, past Windows and killer apps and MS-DOS, all the way to the Altair BASIC.

"And right there is everything about who we are, which is: we create technology so others can create technology," he said in 2017.[25] "Empowering people and organizations all over the planet to achieve more. Every one of those is a key word for us. It's not about our technology, it's about what other people can do with our technology."

" And right there is everything about who we are, which is: we create technology so others can create technology," he said in 2017. "Empowering people and organizations all over the planet to achieve more. Every one of those is a key word for us. It's not about our technology, it's about what other people can do with our technology."

The message was as clear to Nadella as it was to two childhood friends studying a magazine on a drab December day some forty-odd years earlier. The future was here—why not do something special with it?

"At Microsoft we have this very bad habit of not being able to push ourselves because we just feel very self-satisfied with the success we've had. We're learning how not to look at the past."

—SATYA NADELLA,
CEO of Microsoft

CHAPTER EIGHT

KEY ACQUISITIONS

Microsoft's come a long way from its days of computer language. Acquisitions have helped the company deepen its impact in social networking, mobile communications, video games, cloud computing, and computer programming. Here's a look at some of the biggest acquisitions (and one notable investment) Microsoft has made in recent years—and what it's meant for the tech giant.

Facebook

While Microsoft fell behind on mobile and cloud technology, it cashed in on that other pillar of post-2000 tech growth, social media. Just not in the way you think. In October 2007, Microsoft beat out Google to invest in a social media site founded by a former Harvard student, Mark Zuckerberg: Facebook.

Microsoft invested $240 million for a 1.6 percent stake in the start-up.[1] The deal also came with a partnership over third-party advertising.

"We are pleased to take our Microsoft partnership to the next level," Owen Van Natta, chief revenue officer of Facebook, said at the time.[2] "We think this expanded relationship will allow Facebook to continue to innovate and grow as a technology leader and major player in social computing, as well as bring relevant advertising to nearly 50 million active users of Facebook."

While Microsoft never fully capitalized on the advertising side of the deal, and an effort to buy Facebook outright in 2009 failed, it did recoup a healthy return—in the billions—a decade later, by which point Facebook, too, had become one of the world's most successful companies. Consider it a final parting gift from Steve Ballmer's era, a payoff shareholders found easy to "like."

Skype

Microsoft acquired the video conferencing platform in 2011 for $8.5 billion. Skype—which was founded in 2003, bought by eBay in 2005, then later acquired by an investment group—gave Microsoft the leading video conferencing platform. Skype was implemented into programs like Windows 8.1 over Microsoft's own apps. It was eventually transformed to a centralized Azure service and it remains a Microsoft staple nearly a decade after the deal was finalized.

Nokia

Microsoft's 2013 acquisition of the phone maker Nokia's devices and services business reflected the vestiges of Microsoft's old ways of thinking and forced the company to make difficult decisions about its future. Ballmer's pushing through the $7.2 billion deal—against the board's wishes—helped cement his fate at Microsoft. The deal was begrudgingly finalized under Satya Nadella in April 2014. The companies had been longtime partners, and former Microsoft exec Stephen Elop served as Nokia's CEO from 2010 to 2014.

> Microsoft's 2013 acquisition of the phone maker Nokia's devices and services business reflected the vestiges of Microsoft's old ways of thinking and forced the company to make difficult decisions about its future. Ballmer's pushing through the $7.2 billion deal—against the board's wishes—helped cement his fate at Microsoft. The deal was begrudgingly finalized under Satya Nadella in April 2014.

But the acquisition wasn't a good fit. While the Finnish company was shipping more than two hundred million phones a year, its Android-based offerings clashed with Microsoft's

Windows-centric vision. Nokia's reliance on Microsoft apps meant its phones were missing key Google features such as Gmail and Maps. Promising Nokia X phones were scrapped (they ran a version of Android) to make way for Windows Phone products.

Nadella, who had inherited the Nokia situation from former CEO Steve Ballmer, decided to gut Nokia's staff after the acquisition was finalized. Within a few years, Microsoft Mobile sold Nokia phones and wiped its hands clean of the messy purchase.

LinkedIn

Following Microsoft's failed efforts to buy Facebook in 2009, it remained interested in other social media companies. That interest culminated in the acquisition of LinkedIn, the platform for business professionals, for $26.2 billion in June 2016. The site was founded by Reid Hoffman in 2002. The pairing made sense for Microsoft—a brand known for catering to business professionals and a social media platform for business professionals. It was also a chance to follow employees from job to job, beyond their Outlook email accounts. Under Microsoft, LinkedIn has continued to flourish, with a network of five hundred million users and more than $4 billion in revenue during the second half of 2019.

Mojang

Microsoft's 2014 purchase of video game developer Mojang came down to one title: *Minecraft*. The smash hit sandbox game was the centerpiece of the $2.5 billion deal. "Minecraft is more than a great game franchise. It is an open-world platform, driven by a vibrant community we care deeply about, and rich with new opportunities for that community and for Microsoft," Satya Nadella said at the time of the purchase.[3]

Those rich new opportunities have included *Minecraft: Story Mode, Minecraft Classic, Minecraft Earth,* and 2020's *Minecraft Dungeons.* But notably, unlike *Halo* games, which have remained exclusive to Xbox, *Minecraft* games have generally been made available on other platforms such as rival PlayStation.

By late 2019, *Minecraft* had more than 110 million monthly players[4] and the subject of an augmented reality game, *Minecraft Earth*, that blends the world of *Minecraft* overtop the actual world, similarly to *Pokemon Go.*

Github

No acquisition reflects Microsoft's transition quite like that of Github, the software development platform. Former CEOs Bill Gates and Steve Ballmer had both previously railed against open-source during their tenures, but these were different times, and Microsoft was heading in a new direction. The $7.5 billion deal was announced in June 2018. Satya Nadella, in a press release announcing the deal, noted the need to "strengthen our commitment to developer freedom, openness and innovation."

Other Acquisitions

Microsoft's other acquisitions during the past decade have ranged from social networking and software to cloud security and apps. Here are some of the many subsidiaries brought under Microsoft's umbrella:

Social Media

- Yammer, the social networking service, in 2012 for $1.2 billion

Software

- InMage, computer software company, 2014
- Revolution Analytics, statistical software company, in 2015
- VoloMetrix, analytics software company, 2015
- Xamarin, software company, 2016
- AltspaceVR, software start-up, in 2017
- Avere Systems, a tech company, in 2018

Cloud

- Adallom, cloud security company, in 2015 for $320 billion

Apps

- MileIQ, mileage tracking and logging app, 2015

Video Games

Another area of acquisition involved video games—a chance for Microsoft to bolster offerings on the Xbox and PC.

- *Havok—2015*
- *Ninja Theory—2018*
- *Playground Games—2018*

- *Compulsion Games*—2018
- *inXile*—2018
- *Obsidian*—2018
- *Undead Labs*—2018
- *Double Fine*—2019

The Bigger Picture

Acquisitions reveal the extent of Microsoft's growth and a glimpse at the company's vision. Where acquisitions were previously used to plug gaps in Microsoft's offerings (such as aQuantive and Nokia), companies are now being acquired to bolster core strengths. Microsoft has shifted focus significantly from its initial vehicle, the PC, but it needed to shift in order to survive and thrive. Microsoft is also doing a better job of ingraining its acquisitions with its core offerings.

"Things do change, and we've been able to adapt, and have this long-term view, and place multiple strategic bets."

—STEVE CLAYTON,
Chief Storyteller at Microsoft

CHAPTER NINE

MICROSOFT TODAY

Where It Stands, What's New, and a SWOT Analysis

Microsoft is firmly entrenched as one of the world's top companies—a forward-looking tech leader with a range of successful products and a $1 trillion market cap. The company hit that $1 trillion threshold in April 2019, less than a year after Apple and Amazon, and ahead of Google parent Alphabet. By February 2020, Microsoft and Apple were neck and neck in terms of the highest market cap (ranging between $1.36 and $1.4 trillion). Microsoft led Apple between April and October 2019, but slipped to second amid the iPhone 11 release and a broad stock sell-off. Microsoft's stock was up $25 in early 2020, to $185, blasting past analysts' forecasts. Microsoft was ranked fourth in Best Global Brands 2019 by the marketing consultancy firm Interbrand, behind Apple, Google, and Amazon and ahead of Coca-Cola and Samsung.[1]

Various products and revenue streams fuel the company's growth. During the first half of the 2020 fiscal year, total revenue was $69.9 billion, SEC filings reveal[2]—with server products and cloud services ($19.3 billion), office products and cloud services ($17.4 billion), and Windows ($10.9 billion) contributing the bulk of that total. Other significant revenue streams included gaming ($5.8 billion), search advertising ($4.1 billion), and LinkedIn ($4 billion).

Commercial cloud revenue—including Office 365 Commercial, Azure, the commercial portion of LinkedIn, Dynamics 365, and other commercial cloud properties—was $24.1 billion for July–December 2019, up from $17.5 billion for the same time period the previous year.

Cloud

Azure is a central part of the company's outlook and is poised to take Microsoft to new heights in the next decade. While Amazon has maintained the market lead, Microsoft appears to be closing the gap (Microsoft reports total cloud revenue, but doesn't break out the revenue for individual segments such as Azure).

Among large companies, Microsoft—not Amazon—retained a commanding lead in cloud services, a Goldman Sachs survey of tech execs released in January 2020 revealed.[3] Azure also maintains the strongest global cloud network, consisting of 56 regions and available in 140 countries.

Hardware

Hardware is another area where Microsoft is poised to thrive—it's prepared to release a number of new devices in 2020, including the Surface Neo tablet and Surface Duo Android phone, which use dual screens and can be adapted in a number of configurations. And then there's the Xbox Series X, slated for release later in the year, which is twice as powerful as Xbox One, with 120 frames per second gameplay and an SSD drive that should all but eliminate load times.

Other Planned Releases

Microsoft is introducing a new version of Windows, 10X, in the second half of 2020 to pair with its upcoming dual-screen devices. The company revealed new details about Windows 10X at Microsoft 365 Developer Day in February 2020, stating that updates will take less than ninety seconds.[4] Microsoft's other planned releases in 2020 include SharePoint Spaces, an immersive mixed-reality platform; the AI-powered Project Cortex knowledge network; and .NET 5, a unified, open-source programming platform.

Environmental Focus

The company plans to go "carbon negative" by 2030,[5] meaning it will remove more carbon than it emits. And by 2050, Microsoft "will remove from the environment all the carbon the company has emitted either directly or by electrical consumption since it was founded in 1975." The initiative, announced in early 2020, further positions Microsoft as a leader in the tech industry and reflects the company's altruistic ambitions.

Diversity and Inclusion

Microsoft is focused on improving diversity and inclusion. Its first Diversity and Inclusion Report, released in November 2019, showed that 29.2 percent of employees are women, 4.4 percent are Black (up from 4 percent), while 33.3 percent are Asian, up from 32.3 percent the previous year.[6] The report showed the company's gender pay gap was inexistent—women in the US earned $1.001 for every $1.000 earned by their male counterparts, while 88 percent of employees voiced support for Microsoft's efforts at inclusion.

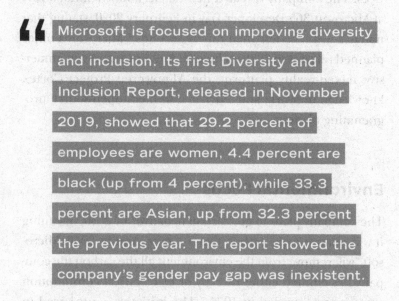

" Microsoft is focused on improving diversity and inclusion. Its first Diversity and Inclusion Report, released in November 2019, showed that 29.2 percent of employees are women, 4.4 percent are black (up from 4 percent), while 33.3 percent are Asian, up from 32.3 percent the previous year. The report showed the company's gender pay gap was inexistent.

The company has also made a commitment to fostering LGBTQI+ inclusion, scoring a 100 score on the Human Rights Campaign's Corporate Equality Index for more than a decade. Microsoft also barred discrimination based on sexual orientation during the 1980s and began offering health benefits to same-sex partners of employees in 1993.

Microsoft SWOT Analysis

Given Microsoft's massive success and widespread popularity, it's important to take a look at the company's standing in 2020 using a SWOT analysis, which includes strengths, weaknesses, opportunities, and threats. While a business's strengths and weaknesses are often internal, the threats and opportunities are usually external in nature.

Microsoft Strengths—Internal Strategic Factors

- Microsoft is among the most respected company brands, and its impact is visible on almost any device, computer, or gaming system.
- Microsoft had $134 billion in cash and short-term investments as of December 2019, giving it the largest cash pile of any company and offering substantial opportunities for mergers and acquisitions and abilities to further build its brand.
- Microsoft has a slate of successful products and software that is readily available and easy to use. Windows 10, for example, is active on more than 900 million devices and available in 190 countries.
- The company attracts some of the best and brightest employees—it receives about two million job applications each year and ranked No. 21 on Glassdoor's Best Places to Work 2020[7] based on

employee reviews. Microsoft has a track record of hiring smart employees with a wide range of expertise.

▪ The current company culture is rooted in a growth mindset, with a focus on continued self-improvement through learning, hard work, and resilience. Microsoft's mission is "to empower every person and every organization on the planet to achieve more."

▪ Organizational changes have reduced obstacles blocking innovation and driven cross-departmental collaborations.

Microsoft Weaknesses—Internal Strategic Factors

▪ Products remain vulnerable to cybercrime and cyberattacks.

▪ Rushed products due to consumer demand or failures in testing protocols can lead to glitch-filled, buggy, or incomplete products reaching market.

▪ Quality or supply problems for hardware can damage brand reputation with issues such as Xbox 360's "Red Ring of Death."

▪ Releases that fall short of sales expectations can undermine the company's success and leave Microsoft overexposed. The issue can be especially problematic in the PC market, where Windows is the industry leader.

▪ Some acquisitions have failed to advance Microsoft's business strategy or come with poor returns.

▪ Given its deep market share and strength in cross-promotion, Microsoft continues to face accusations of monopolistic or anti-competitive practices, such as in January 2020 when an update to

Office 365 ProPlus included a Chrome extension that automatically installed Bing as the default search engine.[8]

- Microsoft contractors or employees are often suspected of listening in on conversations or spying on data, fueling privacy concerns.
- Platforms such as Xbox Live have been used to share threats and harmful content.

Microsoft Opportunities—External Strategic Factors

- Microsoft's Azure cloud product is developing strength in the industry, with nearly 60 percent growth between Q1 fiscal year 2019 and 2020, and is a favorite of many top companies. It's positioned to take market share from Amazon's AWS.
- Microsoft is pursuing innovation through AI projects while also seeking guidelines and regulations to ensure the technology is not misused.
- Partnerships and acquisitions—such as Skype ($8.5 billion), LinkedIn ($26.2 billion), and Github ($7.5 billion)—help to diversify and strengthen Microsoft's reach beyond mainstay offerings like Windows.
- Microsoft is poised to attract new customers with upcoming releases like the Xbox Series X, Surface Neo, and Surface Duo.
- Because of its size and financial flexibility, Microsoft can continue to gain competitive advantages by reducing costs.
- Better penetration into weaker-performing markets could produce new revenue streams. Microsoft leads the operating systems market in Japan (Windows'

market share was above 40 percent in July 2019) but continues to struggle in the video game market, where Sony dominates and Xbox has failed to gain traction with developers. Ollie Barder, writing for *Forbes*, blamed the disconnect in part on cultural issues:

"On the whole, disruptive business practices don't go down well in Japan. Business is more formalized and regulated than in Europe or the US and foreign companies have to learn to work within this framework or fail. . . . Microsoft should have gone in and been more respectful to the cultural framework of gaming in Japan and offered a way to add to it rather than disrupt and replace it outright."[9]

If Microsoft is able to adjust consumer views about the Xbox in Japan, it could open significant growth opportunities.

Microsoft Threats—External Strategic Factors

- Cyberattacks and security vulnerabilities have targeted Microsoft users and pose an ongoing threat. Microsoft has a Digital Crimes Unit devoted to tracking and resolving such issues.
- Low-/no-cost competitors (specifically open-source software) could drive down Microsoft's margins, while piracy results in lost revenue.
- The potential for outages, data losses, and disruptions in services could alienate users and motivate them to become customers of competitors.
- Tech issues and glitches could make customers less likely to use Microsoft products and services.
- Outbreaks like the coronavirus pandemic in 2020

could impact supply chains and cause the company to miss its sales forecasts.

- The company has faced blowback for alienating various groups, such as with Xbox Live in 2009 when it banned gay gamertags (the ban was later lifted).
- Microsoft's competitors pose an ongoing threat as they develop and release services and hardware that could weaken Microsoft's market share.
- Manufacturing issues and delays could diminish sales opportunities. A 2019 PC chip shortage with Intel, for example, weakened sales of Windows and Surface devices.

Geopolitical Factors

Microsoft's global reach and numerous government contracts means the company regularly finds itself ensnared in foreign entanglements and controversial situations that have led to criticism and backlash.

- Employees released an open letter in February 2019 over Microsoft's $480 million contract with the US Army to develop HoloLens headsets. The employees objected to the tools they created being used to "increase lethality."
- Microsoft faced backlash over its contracts with Immigration and Customs Enforcement, the government agency rounding up and detaining undocumented immigrants. Critics worried that the partnership with Microsoft's Azure Government

cloud computing would give ICE access to tools such as facial recognition software Face API, and employees with Microsoft and subsidiary Github published a letter[10] and called for Microsoft to cancel its contracts with ICE, writing that the partnership "makes all of us working at Microsoft complicit to the unethical detainment of tens of thousands of immigrants and the various abuses to which ICE subjects them. Through our technology, we've been contributing to the terrorism of ICE agents on our country's immigrant population and other people of color."

- Microsoft was among the leading tech companies named in a December 2019 class-action lawsuit[11] involving children killed while mining cobalt in the Democratic Republic of the Congo—cobalt is found in lithium-ion batteries.

- Microsoft has clashed numerous times with the European Union, most notably when the European Commission leveled a fine of more than $600 million against the company in 2004 for its "near monopoly" with Windows. The Commission is known to scrutinize new releases, including flagship products such as Windows 10, under competition laws. The arrangements between the EU and Microsoft were also the subject of an inquiry opened by the European Data Protection Supervisor in 2019.[12] Microsoft also sparred over the EU's plan, announced in January 2020, for a temporary ban of facial recognition technology.[13]

- Mistrust between the United States and China could increase production costs by leading to separate supply chains, Satya Nadella admitted in an interview with Bloomberg.[14]

■ A judge in February 2020 halted Microsoft's work on the Pentagon's Joint Enterprise Defense Infrastructure (JEDI) $10 billion cloud contract after Amazon filed a lawsuit alleging that it lost out on the contract due to President Donald Trump's personal vendetta against Amazon CEO Jeff Bezos.

SWOT Analysis—Recommendations

Microsoft's strengths and opportunities far outweigh the many threats facing the company—but it's important for Microsoft to remain vigilant in reducing risk where possible.

Microsoft has been positioning itself as a tech leader ever since Bill Gates and Paul Allen developed their BASIC language for the Altair 8800, and especially after its deal with IBM saw Microsoft licensing MS-DOS computer language. The company's breakout operating system, Windows, and programs like Word and Excel have become worldwide standards, and under CEO Satya Nadella, Microsoft has reestablished itself among the world's most successful companies—and is poised to experience success for years to come.

Some of Microsoft's weaknesses can be diminished with proper attention and caution. Threat protection and safeguards can help to guard against cyberattacks, and additional rounds of testing can reduce the number of bugs or problems in Microsoft's releases. Diligence is needed to ensure that acquisitions further the company's business strategies or will align with Microsoft's structure, instead of simply patching gaps in the company's current offerings.

Opportunities abound for Microsoft. Its Azure cloud and AI offerings are becoming central focuses, and acquisitions will further build Microsoft's reach across various sectors. And upcoming hardware releases could help Microsoft penetrate markets where it's previously struggled.

Microsoft also faces numerous threats, in part because of its size and success, but also because consumer interests and competitor offerings continue to evolve. Competition is everywhere for Microsoft, and its previous delays in adapting to emerging technology—from the internet to search engines and mobile phones—made the company vulnerable and led Microsoft to make risky decisions that damaged the brand, from monopolistic practices in the 1990s to ill-advised acquisitions in the early 2000s.

Microsoft is held to a high standard when it comes to its contracts and should expect blowback when those agreements are not popular ones. The threat of attempted cyberattacks and the potential for geopolitical issues remain high because Microsoft is used so heavily throughout the world in so many countries. Competitors will continue to emerge, both existing and new, with products that mimic and build upon Microsoft's efforts.

In order to remain an industry leader, Microsoft needs to continue looking forward and evolving. The programs and systems that helped fuel Microsoft's rise may one day crater in popularity, but Microsoft has established a pattern of reinventing itself and taking advantage of opportunities that many companies miss or abandon. And even if its initial efforts in a specific field fall short, Microsoft has shown a willingness to stick to a long-term vision and achieve eventual success—a blueprint that stretches from computer language, applications, and operating systems to video games, mobile devices, and cloud computing.

BUSINESS LESSONS AND OPPORTUNITIES

Microsoft rose above the pack in the software industry, disrupted the PC platforms world, developed a winning strategy in video games, and is now positioned to guide innovation well into the twenty-first century with its research division and cloud offerings. Not too shabby for a company that's only had three chief executives in its forty-five years in existence. Along with Apple, Microsoft represents the old guard among tech giants—and in order to stay relevant, Microsoft has had to continually reinvent itself.

Here are the top lessons you can take away from Microsoft's story.

1. Find your purpose. One of Satya Nadella's first acts as CEO was to adjust Microsoft's mission statement: "to empower every person and every organization on the planet to achieve more." Not everyone was buying in to the strategy.

"Initially when that mission statement was coined, I think there was, as you would expect, a level of cynicism around these things, that it's a marketing statement or a throwaway line," said Microsoft Chief Storyteller Steve Clayton. "But we started to do things that made that mission statement very, very real. . . . People were rightly skeptical about how long that mission statement would last. Here we are, six years on, and it still is the most important thing in the company in many ways."

2. Take advantage of opportunities that come your way—they don't always come around twice. When IBM wished to find an operating system for its PC, Bill Gates sent them to Gary Kildall's Digital Research, Inc. But Kildall and IBM struggled to see eye to eye, and IBM returned to Microsoft. Gates wasn't going to let an opportunity like that slip through his fingers again. And the deal with IBM over PC-DOS—in which Microsoft purchased an operating system, then licensed it as MS-DOS to other manufacturers—cemented the company's legacy.

Microsoft could have pigeonholed itself as a computer language company and eventually faded away, but when opportunity arose, it shifted its focus and reinvented itself.

3. In the long run, quality matters more than speed. Other companies have reached market with operating systems, word processor and spreadsheet applications, internet browsers, video game consoles, and cloud computing before Microsoft. At one point, Lotus 1-2-3 was the premiere spreadsheet program, and WordStar and WordPerfect were preferred in word processing, and other graphical user interfaces dominated Windows 1.0. But Microsoft—aided by a healthy financial outlook—remained persistent, improving its releases and finding ways to offer quality or adoption that couldn't be found elsewhere. Microsoft won out because of its solid products, not because it reached the marketplace first. In the case of Xbox, Sony's PlayStation had a half-decade head start and the strength of the best-selling gaming console of all-time. But little by little, over the course of twenty years, Microsoft was able to chip away at Sony's advantage.

4. Innovation means answering questions that haven't been asked. The Altair 8800 that graced the January 1975 cover of *Popular Electronics* presented an opportunity for anyone who saw it: the first moderately priced personal computer that could be available for the masses. This was the chance to buy your own computer. Gates and Allen saw the magazine cover and realized a different opportunity. The computer would need language to run programs and perform tasks—without tightly written language, it wasn't much more than a box with some switches and lights. Anyone else could have written the Altair BASIC, but Gates and Allen jumped at the chance. They saw an opportunity and made the most of it.

5. Partnerships can be advantageous, until they aren't. Microsoft forged its future with two software partnerships during the 1980s: its operating systems for IBM computers, and its programs for Apple. But as the decade wore on, both of those relationships soured as Microsoft pursued its own growth behind Windows. By choosing Windows over OS/2, Microsoft turned its back on its most lucrative partnership, and Microsoft's development of Windows fueled so much animosity that Apple filed a lawsuit. But eventually, Windows won out. Acquiescing to the pressure for the sake of the relationships could have undercut Windows' potential.

6. Learn to work within the system instead of trying to fight it. Microsoft was forced to learn an important lesson through its antitrust case against the Department of Justice. But the lesson almost cost Microsoft everything. As Microsoft's star rose, it took a cavalier attitude about governmental oversight, seeing itself as the engine fueling tech regulation—a gatekeeper policing the industry. It saw Netscape's success with Navigator and decided it was going to "crush" its competitor, putting the weight of its entire range of products and partnerships into that mission. As the case picked up steam, and Microsoft was found in violation of the Sherman Antitrust Act, the company began devoting substantial resources to lobbying, working within the system to exert its influence while avoiding undue attention from the government. Microsoft found it a lot more comfortable being a voice in the government's ear instead of the subject of the government's force.

7. Structure in a way that fosters instead of inhibits innovation. One of the failings of Steve Ballmer's tenure as CEO—and something Satya Nadella has addressed after shifting into the role in 2014—was to knock down the walls between departments and nurture a culture that is less adversarial. Siloing Microsoft's departments diminished innovation and made it difficult for any game-changing products to reach market. Nadella traded corporate meetings for team-building opportunities, refocused resources around growth products, and pivoted the company away from failed mobile strategies.

Mike Maples was similarly able to achieve great success with the applications software division in the 1980s and early 1990s by splitting the department into five units, giving each unit a start-up feel but allowing for standards across the different applications.

8. Be good at more than one thing. Many of the companies Microsoft has overtaken or surpassed—such as Lotus, IBM, and Netscape—developed one standout product. And when other companies entered that space, or when their benchmark products stumbled, the companies struggled to adapt. Diversification has helped Microsoft adjust to industry shifts and weather setbacks. "We don't have one single business that we're reliant upon," Microsoft Chief Storyteller Steve Clayton said. "We've managed to grow completely new multibillion-dollar businesses, and that in some ways insulates you against some of the changes that happen in our industry. Things do change, and we've been able to adapt, and have this long-term view, and place multiple strategic bets."[1]

9. Attract the best and the brightest, and empower them. Microsoft was founded by two college dropouts, and some of its key employees, such as Steve Ballmer, Nathan Myhrvold, and Seamus Blackley, didn't enter the company with a coding background. Other employees found success in various endeavors before shifting to computing and technology. Rob Mallicoat, a senior program manager on the Microsoft Defender Advanced Threat Protection team, previously played professional baseball and pitched for the Houston Astros between 1987 and 1992—he teamed with stars like Nolan Ryan, Craig Biggio, Jeff Bagwell, and Ken Caminiti—before shifting to his second career in the computer industry. Microsoft has attracted many employees with backgrounds in physics, math, and other fields and allowed those employees to pursue innovation, encouraging them to come up with fresh ideas and supporting those ideas to implementation.

10. Do good work, and do good things. In a way, Microsoft's vision continues to follow the path set by its founders, two men who embraced their philanthropic sides and donated billions to meaningful causes. Allen donated more than $2 billion during his lifetime to topics ranging from brain research to restoring ocean health, while the Bill and Melinda Gates Foundation has tackled such topics as infectious disease and waste and sanitation in Third World countries. Microsoft, too, has embraced altruism, donating billions of dollars and partnering with organizations through initiatives like the Hack for Good program. It's also pushed for ethical principles around artificial intelligence so it isn't misused. Being one of the world's richest companies comes with a moral obligation, and Microsoft has made a commitment to give back to the world in meaningful ways.

ENDNOTES

Chapter 1

1. H. Edward Roberts and William Yates, "Altair 8800," *Popular Electronics*, January 1975, americanradiohistory.com/Archive-Poptronics/70s/1975/Poptronics-1975-01.pdf.
2. H. Edward Roberts and William Yates, "Altair 8800."
3. Paul Allen, *Idea Man: A Memoir by the Cofounder of Microsoft* (New York: Penguin Group, 2011), 32–33.
4. Paul Allen, *Idea Man: A Memoir by the Cofounder of Microsoft*, 32–33.
5. Bill Gates interview. National Museum of American History, Smithsonian Institution, americanhistory.si.edu/comphist/gates.htm.
6. "BASIC Begins at Dartmouth," Dartmouth University, dartmouth.edu/basicfifty/basic.html.
7. Paul Allen, *Idea Man: A Memoir by the Cofounder of Microsoft*, 15.
8. *Inside Bill's Brain: Decoding Bill Gates.* Davis Guggenheim, Concordia Studio and Netflix, 2019.
9. *Inside Bill's Brain: Decoding Bill Gates.*
10. Paul Allen, *Idea Man: A Memoir by the Cofounder of Microsoft*, 34–36.
11. Bill Gates interview. National Museum of American History.
12. Bill Gates interview. National Museum of American History.
13. Bill Gates interview. National Museum of American History.
14. Bill Gates interview. National Museum of American History.
15. Bill Gates interview. National Museum of American History.
16. *Inside Bill's Brain: Decoding Bill Gates.*
17. Paul Allen, "Entering a Golden Age of Innovation in Computer Science," March 9, 2017, LinkedIn.com. Accessed at linkedin.com/pulse/entering-golden-age-innovation-computer-science-paul-g-allen/?published=t.

18. *Inside Bill's Brain: Decoding Bill Gates.*

19. Paul Allen, *Idea Man: A Memoir by the Cofounder of Microsoft,* 54–55.

20. Paul Allen, *Idea Man: A Memoir by the Cofounder of Microsoft,* 54–55.

21. Bill Gates interview. National Museum of American History.

22. *Inside Bill's Brain: Decoding Bill Gates.*

23. Bill Gates interview. National Museum of American History.

24. Paul Allen, *Idea Man: A Memoir by the Cofounder of Microsoft,* 56.

25. Paul Allen, *Idea Man: A Memoir by the Cofounder of Microsoft,* 56.

26. Paul Allen, *Idea Man: A Memoir by the Cofounder of Microsoft,* 56.

27. Paul Allen, *Idea Man: A Memoir by the Cofounder of Microsoft,* 56.

28. Paul Allen, *Idea Man: A Memoir by the Cofounder of Microsoft,* 56.

29. "ALTAIR BASIC—UP AND RUNNING," *Computer Notes,* April 7, 1975, altairclone.com/downloads/computer_notes/1975_01 _01.pdf.

30. Paul Allen, *Idea Man: A Memoir by the Cofounder of Microsoft,* 86.

31. "Microsoft Fast Facts: 1975," Microsoft, May 9, 2000, news .microsoft.com/2000/05/09/microsoft-fast-facts-1975/.

32. Bill Gates, "An Open Letter to Hobbyists," February 3, 1976, DigiBarn, digibarn.com/collections/newsletters/homebrew /V2_01/homebrew_V2_01_p2.jpg.

33. Harry McCracken, "15 Ways Microsoft Can Reinvent Itself for the Post-Gates Era," *PCWorld,* June 25, 2008, pcworld.com/article /147558/microsoft.html.

34. Paul Allen, *Idea Man: A Memoir by the Cofounder of Microsoft,* 102.

35. Paul Allen, *Idea Man: A Memoir by the Cofounder of Microsoft,* 102.

36. Paul Allen, *Idea Man: A Memoir by the Cofounder of Microsoft,* 102.

37. Paul Allen, *Idea Man: A Memoir by the Cofounder of Microsoft,* 102.

38. Robert X. Cringely, *Triumph of the Nerds,* PBS, 1995, pbs.org /nerds/part2.html.

39. Mug Shots: Bill Gates, The Smoking Gun, www.thesmokinggun .com/mugshots/celebrity/business/bill-gates.

40. Matt Weinberger, "WHERE ARE THEY NOW? What Happened to the People in Microsoft's Iconic 1978 Company Photo," *Business Insider,* January 26, 2019, businessinsider.com/microsoft -1978-photo-2016-10.

41. "History of Microsoft," *Los Angeles Times,* April 4, 2000, latimes .com/archives/la-xpm-2000-apr-04-fi-15769-story.html.

42. Paul Allen, *Idea Man: A Memoir by the Cofounder of Microsoft*, 124.
43. "Meet the inventor of the electronic spreadsheet | Dan Bricklin," Ted, February 1, 2017, YouTube, youtube.com/watch?v=YD vbDiJZpy0.
44. Dan Bricklin, "Patents and Software," Dan Bricklin's website, bricklin.com/patentsandsoftware.htm.
45. Paul Allen, *Idea Man: A Memoir by the Cofounder of Microsoft*.
46. Emmie Martin, "9 Billionaires Who Drive Cheap Hondas, Toyotas and Chevrolets," CNBC, August 21, 2018, cnbc.com/2018/08 /21/9-billionaires-who-still-drive-cheap-hondas-toyotas-and -chevrolets.html.
47. Paul Allen, *Idea Man: A Memoir by the Cofounder of Microsoft*, 131–32.

Chapter 2

1. *Inside Bill's Brain: Decoding Bill Gates*.
2. "Mary Gates, 64; Helped Her Son Start Microsoft," Associated Press, June 11, 1994, nytimes.com/1994/06/11/obituaries/mary -gates-64-helped-her-son-start-microsoft.html.
3. Robert X. Cringely, *Triumph of the Nerds*.
4. Robert X. Cringely, *Triumph of the Nerds*.
5. Robert X. Cringely, *Triumph of the Nerds*.
6. Paul Allen, *Idea Man: A Memoir by the Cofounder of Microsoft*, 128.
7. Jimmy Maher, "The Complete History of the IBM PC, Part Two: The DOS Empire Strikes," *Arts Technica*, July 31, 2017, arstechnica .com/gadgets/2017/07/ibm-pc-history-part-2/.
8. Paul Allen, *Idea Man: A Memoir by the Cofounder of Microsoft*, 143.
9. Jeffrey Young, "Could-A-Beens," *Forbes*, July 7, 1997, accessed at Nexis.com.
10. Jeffrey Young, "Could-A-Beens."
11. "Gary Kildall; His Software System Lost to Rival MS-DOS," *Los Angeles Times*, July 15, 1994, latimes.com/archives/la-xpm-1994 -07-15-mn-15775-story.html.
12. Paul Allen, *Idea Man: A Memoir by the Cofounder of Microsoft*, 137–40.
13. Paul Allen, *Idea Man: A Memoir by the Cofounder of Microsoft*, 137–40.
14. James Wallace and Jim Erickson, *Hard Drive* (New York: John Wiley & Sons, 1992), 138.

15. James Wallace and Jim Erickson, *Hard Drive*, 138.
16. Paul Allen, *Idea Man: A Memoir by the Cofounder of Microsoft*, 160–62.
17. Bill Gates interview. National Museum of American History.
18. Benj Edwards, "Microsoft Word Turns 25," *PC World*, October 22, 2008, pcworld.com/article/152585/microsoft_word_program.html.
19. Bill Gates interview. National Museum of American History.
20. David Bunnell, "Polishing the Mac," *Macworld*, April 1984, https://archive.org/details/MacWorld8404April1984Premier/mode/2up.
21. "1983 Apple Event Bill Gates and Steve Jobs," YouTube, youtube.com/watch?v=NVtxEA7AEHg.
22. "When Steve Met Bill: 'It Was a Kind of Weird Seduction Visit,'" *Fortune*, October 24, 2011, fortune.com/2011/10/24/when-steve-met-bill-it-was-a-kind-of-weird-seduction-visit/.
23. Tom Maremaa, "Microsoft Strikes First in War against Lotus," *InfoWorld*, May 27, 1985, books.google.com/books?id=4y4EAAAAMBAJ&pg=PA28&dq="MICROSOFT"%2B"IBM"%2B"MACINTOSH"%2B"GATES"&hl=en&sa=X&ved=2ahUKEwjgkebl19zmAhW3B50JHc29Dz8Q6AEwAXoECAEQAw#v=onepage&q="MICROSOFT"%2B"IBM"%2B"MACINTOSH"%2B"GATES"&f=false.
24. "When Steve Met Bill: 'It Was a Kind of Weird Seduction Visit.'"
25. Scott Olster, "Inside the Deal That Made Bill Gates $350,000,000," *Fortune*, March 13, 2011, fortune.com/2011/03/13/inside-the-deal-that-made-bill-gates-350000000/.
26. John Gantz, "Microsoft: Is Company at the Crest of Glory?" *InfoWorld*, March 17, 1986, books.google.com/books?id=lC8EAAAAMBAJ&pg=PA21&lpg=PA21&dq="The+company+is+clearly+well-run,+well-financed,+and+well-respected"&source=bl&ots=3KDOJYlf-7&sig=ACfU3U3g8mhsXZOqNjIilIpWUTzP_fYrgw&hl=en&sa=X&ved=2ahUKEwjH2qnsod_nAhX2lHIEHbAhBnQQ6AEwAHoECAEQAQ#v=onepage&q="The%20company%20is%20clearly%20well-run%2C%20well-financed%2C%20and%20well-respected"&f=false.
27. Bill Gates interview. National Museum of American History.
28. Dan Farber. "Mitch Kapor Remembers Lotus' Macintosh Bomb," Cnet, January 23, 2014, cnet.com/news/mitch-kapor-remembers-lotus-macintosh-bomb/.

29. John Walkenbach, "Microsoft's PC Spreadsheet Sets New Standard," *InfoWorld*, December 21, 1987, https://books.google.com /books?id=AT8EAAAAMBAJ&pg=PA41&lpg=PA41&dq=%2522 one+of+the+year%2527s+most+innovative+products,+more +powerful+and+more+forward+looking+than+any+other +spreadsheet+on+the+market%2522&source=bl&ots=Pmf 3FIphfk&sig=ACfU3U2Ky6fK7urwLQgKVfw2tQ7TPkyhqA&hl =en&sa=X&ved=2ahUKEwj-5ObqlpDnAhXtV98KHSXyCqk Q6AEwAHoECAYQAQ#v=onepage&q=%2522one%2520 of%2520the%2520year's%2520most%2520innovative%2520 products%252C%2520more%2520powerful%2520and%2520 more%2520forward%2520looking%2520than%2520any%2520 other%2520spreadsheet%2520on%2520the%2520market %2522&f=false.

30. Victor F. Zonana, "Cocky Microsoft Set to Challenge Software Rivals on Their Own Turf," *Los Angeles Times*, August 23, 1987, latimes.com/archives/la-xpm-1987-08-23-fi-3149-story.html.

31. Nick Arnett and Scott Palmer, "Gates Challenges Apple Copyright Claims, Citing Licensing Agreement," *InfoWorld*, March 28, 1988, books.google.com/books?id=6T4EAAAAMBAJ&pg=PA1 &lpg=PA1&dq="We're+saying+that+these+graphic+interface +techniques,+the+ideas,+are+not+copyrightable"&source=bl &ots=r2FdL4ZhS3&sig=ACfU3U05TNq3ChcR3qhXxdu4VIXrm JmaSw&hl=en&sa=X&ved=2ahUKEwiNw62Opd_nAhUWl3IE HYUuDmkQ6AEwAHoECAoQAQ#v=onepage&q="We're%20 saying%20that%20these%20graphic%20interface%20techniques %2C%20the%20ideas%2C%20are%20not%20copyrightable"& f=false.

32. James Coates, "Microsoft's 'Adult,' 52, to retire," *Chicago Tribune*, May 16, 1995, chicagotribune.com/news/ct-xpm-1995-05-16 -9505160254-story.html.

33. Victor F. Zonana, "Microsoft's Applications Software Unit Split into 5," *Los Angeles Times*, September 2, 1998, accessed at Nexis .com; Stuart J. Johnston and Rachel Parker, "Microsoft Splits Application Group," *InfoWorld*, September 5, 1988, books.google .com/books?id=gjoEAAAAMBAJ&pg=PA3&lpg=PA3&dq ="microsoft"%2B"office+business"%2B"graphics+business" %2B"entry+business"%2B"data+access+business"%2B"analysis +business+unit"&source=bl&ots=4hgruN_uQD&sig=ACfU3U3

pZr1N_1Rt5vlH5bjRc8yfGfjfAw&hl=en&sa=X&ved=2ahUKE
wjWuPfvzObnAhXhknIEHQAlD1kQ6AEwAXoECAoQAQ#v
=onepage&q="microsoft"%2B"office%20business"%2B"graphics
%20business"%2B"entry%20business"%2B"data%20access%20
business"%2B"analysis%20business%20unit"&f=false.

34. Stuart J. Johnston and Rachel Parker, "Microsoft Splits Application Group."

35. "140: Mike Maples, Sr.—Microsoft Legend | Legends & Losers Podcast," December 10, 2018, YouTube, youtube.com/watch?v=IHjDxy1Czys.

36. Mario Juarez, telephone interview with author, December 2019.

37. Mario Juarez, telephone interview with author.

38. Mario Juarez, telephone interview with author.

39. Mario Juarez, telephone interview with author.

40. "An Illustrated History of Microsoft Windows," Tower, git-tower.com/blog/history-of-microsoft-windows/.

41. Mario Juarez, telephone interview with author.

42. Bob Metcalfe, "Is Microsoft Abusing Its Power?" *ComputerWorld*, February 25, 1991. Accessed on Nexis.com.

43. *United States of America v. Microsoft Corporation*, Memorandum Opinion No. 94-1564 (D.D.C. 1995).

44. Crystal Jones, "Bill and Melinda Gates," Learning to Give, learningtogive.org/resources/bill-and-melinda-gates.

45. Crystal Jones, "Bill and Melinda Gates."

Chapter 3

1. Michele Matassa Flores, Stanley Holmes, and Laura Benko, "Winding for Windows 95," *Seattle Times*, August 24, 1995, accessed at Nexis.com.

2. "Microsoft Windows 95 Launch Footage," YouTube, youtube.com/watch?v=y0CRWAz09r8.

3. "Windows 95 'Start Me Up' Commercial 1080p Restored," YouTube, youtube.com/watch?v=BNzWyQPIpVg.

4. "Windows 95 Video Guide with Matthew Perry & Jennifer Aniston," YouTube, youtube.com/watch?v=fXpfdq3WYu4.

5. Jordan Runtagh, "Weezer's Blue Album: 10 Things You Didn't Know," *Rolling Stone*, May 10, 2019, rollingstone.com/music

/music-features/weezer-blue-album-rivers-cuomo-things-you -didnt-know-822881/.

6. Jonathan Chew, "Microsoft Launched This Product 20 Years Ago and Changed the World," *Fortune*, August 24, 2015, fortune.com /2015/08/24/20-years-microsoft-windows-95/.

7. Julie Pitta, "PC Industry Likes Everything About Windows 95 Except the Competition: Retailing: Other companies are making products for Windows 95, but Microsoft retains a significant lead," *Los Angeles Times*, August 20, 1995, latimes.com /archives/la-xpm-1995-08-20-fi-37014-story.html.

8. Nathan Myhrvold, phone interview with the author, January 2020.

9. Harry McCracken, "On This Day 22 Years Ago, Bill Gates Wrote His Legendary 'Internet Tidal Wave' Memo," *Fast Company*, May 26, 2017, fastcompany.com/4039009/22-years-ago-today-bill-gates -wrote-his-legendary-internet-tidal-wave-memo.

10. Matt Blitz, "Later, Navigator: How Netscape Won and Then Lost the World Wide Web," *Popular Mechanics*, April 4, 2019, popularmechanics.com/culture/web/a27033147/netscape -navigator-history/.

11. "Netscape's Marc Andreessen," *Time*, February 19, 1996, content .time.com/time/covers/0,16641,19960219,00.html.

12. "Netscape CEO Barksdale's Deposition in Microsoft Suit," Bloomberg, October 21, 1998, bloomberg.com/press-releases /1998-10-21/netscape-ceo-barksdale-s-deposition-in-microsoft -suit-text.

13. "Netscape CEO Barksdale's Deposition in Microsoft Suit."

14. "Spyglass Reports a Net Loss, Ends Dispute with Microsoft," *Wall Street Journal*, January 22, 1997, wsj.com/articles/SB85395 1556366245500.

15. Howard Wolinsky, "How Spyglass Survived Microsoft Deal," *Chicago Sun-Times*, January 11, 1999, accessed at Nexis.com.

16. "America Celebrates Microsoft Bob Day," PR Newswire, March 31, 1995, accessed at Nexis.com.

17. Robinson Meyer, "Even Early Focus Groups Hated Clippy," *Atlantic*, June 23, 2015, theatlantic.com/technology/archive /2015/06/clippy-the-microsoft-office-assistant-is-the-patriarchys -fault/396653/.

18. "Microsoft Office XP Ad 1/3—Clippy Gets Clipped," YouTube, youtube.com/watch?v=tu_Pzuwy-JY.

19. David Lumb, "A Brief History of AOL," *Fast Company*, May 12, 2015, fastcompany.com/3046194/a-brief-history-of-aol.

20. "Electronic Arts Acquires DreamWorks Interactive from Microsoft and DreamWorks SKG," PR Newswire, February 24, 2000, accessed at Nexis.com.

21. Joseph Knoop, "How a Failed Jurassic Park Game Led to the Creation of the Xbox," IGN, May 14, 2018, ign.com/articles /2018/05/14/how-a-failed-jurassic-park-game-led-to-the -creation-of-the-xbox-a-ign-unfiltered.

22. Andrew Sanchez, "Trespasser," *Maximum PC*, January 1999, books.google.com/books?id=IgIAAAAAMBAJ&pg=PP92&lpg =PP92&dq=dreamworks+trespasser&source=bl&ots=Ss40lzY7Xi &sig=ACfU3U2DBjfryHlHH60sKd2Tw2z55t8tmw&hl=en&sa=X &ved=2ahUKEwiXrt6K-urmAhWOY98KHbEAAQ84Ch DoATADegQIChAC#v=onepage&q=dreamworks%20trespasser &f=false.

23. Robert X. Cringely, *Triumph of the Nerds*.

24. Yoni Heisler, "What Ever Became of Microsoft's $150 Million Investment in Apple?" Engadget, May 20, 2014, engadget.com /2014/05/20/what-ever-became-of-microsofts-150-million -investment-in-apple/.

25. Joseph Nocera, "I Remember Microsoft," *Fortune*, July 10, 2000, money.cnn.com/magazines/fortune/fortune_archive/2000 /07/10/283772/index.htm.

26. Satya Nadella, *Hit Refresh* (New York: Harper Business, 2017).

Chapter 4

1. "USA: Attorney General Janet Reno Microsoft Press Conference," AP Archive, YouTube, youtube.com/watch?v=pxtBJxvgHV0.

2. "Justice Department Files Antitrust Suit against Microsoft for Unlawfully Monopolizing Computer Software Markets," May 18, 1998, justice.gov/archive/atr/public/press_releases/1998 /1764.htm.

3. Nathan Myhrvold, phone interview with author, January 2020.

4. "Record Penalty Sought for Firm; Justice Department Wants Microsoft Fined $1 Million a Day; Monopoly Abuse Charged; Re-

quiring Windows Licensees to Install Browser Called Illegal,"
Associated Press, October 21, 1997, accessed at Nexis.com.

5. *United States of America v. Microsoft Corporation*, Supplemental to
Civil Action No. 94-1564 (D.D.C. 1997).

6. *United States of America v. Microsoft Corporation*, RESPONSE OF
THE UNITED STATES TO APPELLANT MICROSOFT COR-
PORATION'S MOTION FOR A STAY OF THE PRELIMINARY
INJUNCTION INSOFAR AS IT RELATES TO WINDOWS 98
No. 97-5343 (D.D.C. 1998).

7. Paul Tharp, "Pie Plot on Gates Was an Inside Lob," *New York Post*,
February 13, 1998, accessed at Nexis.com.

8. "IDC Study Reveals U.S. Browser Market Share Shifts as Microsoft Makes Gains, AOL Remains Stable, and Netscape Drops,"
IDG, September 28, 1998, https://www.idg.com/news/idc-study
-reveals-u-s-browser-market-share-shifts-as-microsoft-makes-gains
-aol-remains-stable-and-netscape-drops/.

9. Nathan Myhrvold, phone interview with the author, January 2020.

10. "Excerpts from Bill Gates's Deposition in Microsoft Antitrust
Trial," *Washington Post*, November 3, 1998, accessed at Nexis
.com.

11. James V. Grimaldi, "Microsoft Trial—The Gates Deposition: 684
Pages of Conflict," *Seattle Times*, March 16, 1999, archive.seattle-
times.com/archive/?date=19990316&slug=2949718.

12. *U.S. v. Microsoft*, Proposed findings of fact, justice.gov/atr/us
-v-microsoft-proposed-findings-fact-0.

13. Rajiv Chandrasekaran, "Microsoft Assailed in Court," *Washington
Post*, October 20, 1998, washingtonpost.com/wp-srv/business
/longterm/microsoft/stories/1998/assails102098.htm.

14. "OEMs and the Internet," email by Bill Gates, January 5, 1996,
web.archive.org/web/20000816224323/http://www.usdoj.gov
/atr/cases/exhibits/295.pdf.

15. "The Internet PC," Bill Gates email, April 10, 1996, web.archive
.org/web/20000816224824/http://www.usdoj.gov/atr/cases
/exhibits/336.pdf.

16. Joel Brinkley, "As Microsoft Trial Gets Started, Gates's Credibil-
ity Is Questioned," *New York Times*, October 20, 1998, nytimes
.com/library/tech/98/10/biztech/articles/20microsoft.html.

17. Andrew Zajac, "Microsoft Strikes Underdog Pose," *Chicago Tribune*, October 21, 1998, accessed at Nexis.com.

18. *U.S. v. Microsoft*, Direct Testimony of Jim Barksdale, Civil Action No. 98-1232 (D.D.C. 1998).

19. *U.S. v. Microsoft*, Direct Testimony of Jim Barksdale.

20. *U.S. v. Microsoft*, Direct Testimony of Jim Barksdale.

21. *U.S. v. Microsoft*, Direct Testimony of Jim Barksdale.

22. Ben Slivka email to Bill Gates, April 14, 1997, justice.gov/sites /default/files/atr/legacy/2006/03/03/58.pdf.

23. Rajiv Chandrasekaran, "Gates Escalates PR War Outside Court," *Washington Post*, December 8, 1998, accessed at Nexis.com.

24. *U.S. v. Microsoft*, Court's findings of fact, Civil Action No. 98-1232 (D.D.C. 1998).

25. *U.S. v. Microsoft*, Court's findings of fact.

26. "Bill Gates Promotes Steve Ballmer to President and CEO," PR Newswire, January 13, 2000, accessed at Nexis.com.

27. Nathan Myhrvold, phone interview with the author, January 2020.

28. *U.S. v. Microsoft*, Conclusions of Law, Civil Action No. 98-1232 (D.D.C. 2000).

29. Michael J. Martinez, "Microsoft to Fight Breakup Order," Associated Press, June 8, 2000. Accessed at Nexis.com.

30. "Judge: Gates a Napoleon," ABC News, January 8, 2001, abcnews.go.com/Technology/story?id=99269&page=1.

Chapter 5

1. Dean Takahashi, "Microsoft Joins the Game: Announces Plan to Take on Nintendo, Sony and Sega with the X-Box," *Montreal Gazette*, March 11, 2000, accessed at Nexis.com.

2. "Macworld 1999," YouTube, youtube.com/watch?v=Gw3Vl nQ cTns.

3. Todd Bishop, "How Steve Jobs Reacted to Microsoft's Bungie Acquisition," GeekWire, December 5, 2011, geekwire.com/2011 /steve-jobs-reacted-microsofts-bungie-acquisition/.

4. Howard Wolinsky, "Microsoft Acquires Gamemaker," *Chicago Sun-Times*, June 19, 2000, accessed at Nexis.com.

5. Dean Takahashi, phone interview with the author, January 2020.

6. John Markoff, "Microsoft's $1 Billion Bet on Xbox Network," *New York Times*, May 20, 2002, nytimes.com/2002/05/20 /business/microsoft-s-1-billion-bet-on-xbox-network.html.

7. John Markoff, "Microsoft's \$1 Billion Bet on Xbox Network."

8. Tor Thorsen, "Xbox 360 Failure Rate 23.7%, PS3 10%, Wii 2.7%—Study," GameSpot, September 2, 2009, web.archive.org /web/20090906005326/http:/www.gamespot.com/news /6216691.html.

9. Ryan McCaffrey, "Podcast Unlocked 201: Xbox Bosses Past and Present Share Stories, Secrets," IGN, July 1, 2015, uk.ign.com /articles/2015/07/02/podcast-unlocked-201-xbox-bosses-past -and-present-share-stories-secrets?+hub+page+%28front+page %29&utm_content=2.

10. Mike Plant, "Top 10 Best-selling Videogame Consoles," Guinness World Records, December 21, 2018, guinnessworldrecords.com /news/2018/12/top-10-best-selling-videogame-consoles-551938/.

11. "Kinect for Xbox 360 Sets the Future in Motion—No Controller Required," PR Newswire, June 14, 2010, accessed at Nexis.com.

12. "Kinect Confirmed as Fastest-Selling Consumer Electronics Device," Guinness World Records, March 3, 2011, web.archive .org/web/20110311213211/http:/community.guinnessworld records.com/_Kinect-Confirmed-As-Fastest-Selling-Consumer -Electronics-Device/blog/3376939/7691.html.

13. Ian Sherr, "Microsoft and Sony Diverge on Gaming 'Cloud,'" *Wall Street Journal*, May 22, 2013, blogs.wsj.com/digits/2013 /05/22/microsoft-and-sony-diverge-on-gaming-cloud/?utm _source=buffer&utm_medium=twitter&utm_campaign=Buffer &utm_content=buffer94b3f.

14. Eddie Makuch, "GTA 5 Reaches Impressive New Sales Milestone, as Microtransaction Spending Grows," Gamespot, February 6, 2020, gamespot.com/articles/gta-5-reaches-impressive-new -sales-milestone-as-mi/1100-6473475/.

Chapter 6

1. "Steve Ballmer Going Crazy on Stage," YouTube, youtube.com /watch?v=I14b-C67EXY.

2. "TechLive—Windows XP: The End of the MS-DOS Era," You-Tube, youtube.com/watch?v=A-HIlNGczgU.

3. Bill and Melinda Gates, "Why We Swing for the Fences," Gates-Notes, February 10, 2020, gatesnotes.com/2020-Annual-Letter

?WT.mc_id=20200210000000_AL2020_BG-FB_&WT.tsrc=BGFB &fbclid=IwAR0ozkhh5wHGPJrgJ5vN69apRCOCo5VedGw3Zk 2X81tal2vJpjCY7gaKgqU.

4. "The European Commission's Decision in the Microsoft Case and its Implications for Other Companies and Industries," Microsoft, April 2004, http://download.microsoft.com/download /5/2/7/52794f65-8784-43cf-8651-c7d9e7d34f90/Comment on EC Microsoft Decision.pdf.

5. Fred Vogelstein, "The Day Google Had to 'Start Over' on Android," *Atlantic*, December 18, 2013, theatlantic.com /technology/archive/2013/12/the-day-google-had-to-start -over-on-android/282479/.

6. "Ballmer on Microsoft Pt. 1," CNBC, January 17, 2007, cnbc .com/video/2007/01/17/ballmer-on-microsoft-pt-1.html.

7. "Ballmer on Microsoft Pt. 1."

8. Terry Myerson, "Thank You for 21 Years, and Onto the Next Chapter . . ." LinkedIn, March 29, 2018, linkedin.com/pulse /thank-you-21-years-onto-next-chapter-terry-myerson/.

9. Brad Molen, "Windows Phone 8 review," Engadget, October 29, 2012, engadget.com/2012/10/29/windows-phone-8-review/.

10. "Top 15 Funniest 'Get a Mac' Ads," YouTube, youtube.com /watch?v=1rV-dbDMS18.

11. "Ex-Microsoft CEO Steve Ballmer Talks U.S. Election, Working with Bill Gates & More," Bloomberg, November 6, 2016, youtube .com/watch?v=nwNNlFLOWME.

12. "Bing at Build 2013: Weaving an Intelligent Fabric," *Bing blogs*, June 28, 2013, blogs.bing.com/canada/2013/06/28/bing-at -build-2013-weaving-an-intelligent-fabric.

13. Satya Nadella, *Hit Refresh*, 47.

14. Mario Juarez, phone interview with the author, December 2019.

Chapter 7

1. "Satya Nadella Is Microsoft's New CEO," YouTube, February 5, 2014, youtube.com/watch?v=euwe50Bh9MM.

2. "Satya Nadella Is Microsoft's New CEO."

3. Satya Nadella, *Hit Refresh*, 1.

4. Janet I. Tu, "Hackathon Sets Tone for the New Microsoft," *Seattle Times*, July 30, 2014, accessed at Nexis.com.

5. Janet I. Tu, "Hackathon Sets Tone for the New Microsoft."

6. Austin Carr and Dina Bass, "The Most Valuable Company (for Now) Is Having a Nadellaissance," Bloomberg, May 2, 2019, bloomberg.com/news/features/2019-05-02/satya-nadella -remade-microsoft-as-world-s-most-valuable-company.

7. Mario Juarez, phone interview with the author, December 2019.

8. Satya Nadella, *Hit Refresh*, 61.

9. Steven Martin, "Upcoming Name Change for Windows Azure," *Microsoft Azure Blog*, March 24, 2014, azure.microsoft.com/en -us/blog/upcoming-name-change-for-windows-azure.

10. Scott Hanselman, "Microsoft Killed My Pappy," February 22, 2014, hanselman.com/blog/MicrosoftKilledMyPappy.aspx.

11. Immo Landwerth, ".NET Core is Open Source," November 12, 2014, devblogs.microsoft.com/dotnet/net-core-is-open-source/.

12. "Contribute to Microsoft Open Source Projects," Microsoft, opensource.microsoft.com.

13. "Microsoft Loves Linux," *Windows Server Blog*, May 6, 2015, cloudblogs.microsoft.com/windowsserver/2015/05/06 /microsoft-loves-linux/.

14. The Linux Foundation, linuxfoundation.org.

15. "Microsoft CFO Amy Hood on Purpose and Progression," Finding Mastery, findingmastery.net/amy-hood/?fbclid=IwAR1Zjlg ZNh_CMzdRgNX7cvJe379c0O6W83bNo3lcpmvK8rqGaaXrgm KJvdU.

16. Satya Nadella, *Hit Refresh*, 82.

17. Steve Clayton, phone interview with the author, February 2020.

18. "Desktop Windows Version Market Share Worldwide," Statcounter, gs.statcounter.com/windows-version-market-share /desktop/worldwide/#monthly-201701-201911.

19. "Second Quarter Form 10Q," Microsoft SEC Filings, microsoft .com/en-us/Investor/sec-filings.aspx.

20. "What Is Azure?" Microsoft Azure, azure.microsoft.com/en-us /overview/what-is-azure/.

21. Bill Gates, "The Side of Paul Allen I Wish More People Knew About," GatesNotes, June 28, 2019, gatesnotes.com/About -Bill-Gates/Forbes-Philanthropy-Summit-honors-Paul-Allen.

22. Youyou Zhou, "Thirty Years of Financial Filings Reveal Microsoft's Biggest Competitors," Quartz, February 20, 2019, qz.com/1553700 /this-30-year-timeline-reveals-microsofts-biggest-competitors/.

23. Satya Nadella, *Hit Refresh*, 125.
24. Ina Fried, "Microsoft, Google Agree to Stop Complaining to Regulators about Each Other," Recode, April 22, 2016, vox .com/2016/4/22/11586336/microsoft-google-agree-to-stop -complaining-to-regulators-about-each.
25. Steve Ranger, "Why Does Microsoft Exist? How CEO Satya Nadella Answered the Tech Giant's Existential Question," ZDNet, October 3, 2017, zdnet.com/article/why-does-microsoft-exist -how-ceo-satya-nadella-answered-the-tech-giants-existential -question/.

Chapter 8

1. Robert A. Guth, "Microsoft Bets on Facebook Stake and Web Ad Boom," Associated Press, October 25, 2007, accessed at Nexis .com.
2. "Facebook and Microsoft Expand Strategic Alliance," October 24, 2007, web.archive.org/web/20090124172049/https:/www .microsoft.com/Presspass/press/2007/oct07/10-24Facebook PR.mspx.
3. Mia Shanley and Bill Rigby, "Microsoft to Buy Minecraft Maker Mojang for $2.5 billion," Reuters, September 15, 2014, reuters .com/article/microsoft-mojang/microsoft-to-buy-minecraft -maker-mojang-for-2-5-billion-idINKBN0HA1DD20140915.
4. Ben Gilbert, "'Minecraft' Has Been Quietly Dominating for Over 10 Years, and Now Has 112 Million Players Every Month," *Business Insider*, September 14, 2019, businessinsider.com /minecraft-monthly-player-number-microsoft-2019-9.

Chapter 9

1. "Best Global Brands 2019," Interbrand, interbrand.com/best -brands/best-global-brands/2019/ranking/.
2. Microsoft SEC Filings, microsoft.com/en-us/Investor/sec -filings.aspx.
3. Naomi Eide, "Enterprise-Scale Companies Adopting Azure over AWS, Goldman Sachs Finds," CIODive, January 10, 2020, ciodive

.com/news/Microsoft-Azure-AWS-IaaS-Cloud/570170/?_lrsc
=2fbc6db0-c3a4-4a99-aa71-96786a7c62e4.

4. Tom Warren, "Microsoft Promises Windows 10X updates Will
Take 'Less Than 90 Seconds,'" The Verge, February 11, 2020,
theverge.com/2020/2/11/21133272/microsoft-windows-10x
-windows-updates-fast-speed-details.

5. Brad Smith, "Microsoft Will Be Carbon Negative by 2030," *Official Microsoft Blog,* January 16, 2020, blogs.microsoft.com/blog
/2020/01/16/microsoft-will-be-carbon-negative-by-2030/.

6. "Diversity and Inclusion Report," Microsoft, November 2019,
query.prod.cms.rt.microsoft.com/cms/api/am/binary/RE4
aqv1.

7. "Best Places to Work 2020," Glassdoor, glassdoor.com/Award
/Best-Places-to-Work-LST_KQ0,19.htm.

8. Paul Thurrott, "Microsoft to Push Bing on Office 365 ProPlus
Customers," January 22, 2020, thurrott.com/cloud/office-365
/228606/microsoft-to-push-bing-on-office-365-proplus
-customers.

9. Ollie Barder, "The Real Reasons Why the Xbox Continues to
Fail in Japan," *Forbes,* December 30, 2019, forbes.com/sites
/olliebarder/2020/12/30/the-real-reasons-why-the-xbox
-continues-to-fail-in-japan/#27edbe924efa.

10. "Microsoft Workers Stand in Solidarity with Githubbers in Their
Demands to Cancel Their Contract with ICE," Gitbub, github
.com/MSWorkers/support.Githubbers.

11. Morgan Winsor, "Apple, Google, Microsoft, Dell, Tesla Sued
over Deaths of Child Miners," ABC News, December 18, 2019,
abcnews.go.com/International/apple-google-microsoft-dell
-tesla-named-lawsuit-deaths/story?id=67795965.

12. Natasha Lomas, "EU Contracts with Microsoft Raising 'Serious'
Data Concerns, Says Watchdog," Techcrunch, October 21, 2019,
techcrunch.com/2019/10/21/eu-contracts-with-microsoft
-raising-serious-data-concerns-says-watchdog/.

13. "Google and Microsoft Spar over EU Plan to Ban Facial Recognition," Reuters, January 20, 2020, venturebeat.com/2020
/01/20/google-and-microsoft-spar-over-eu-plan-to-ban-facial
-recognition/.

14. Dina Bass and Amy Thomson, "Microsoft CEO Says U.S.-China Spat May Hurt Global Growth and Warns That Countries That Fail to Attract Immigrants Will Lose Out," Bloomberg, January 21, 2020, seattletimes.com/business/microsoft-ceo-says-u-s-china -spat-may-hurt-global-growth/.

Business Lessons and Opportunities

1. Steve Clayton, phone interview with the author, February 2020.

INDEX

THE
DOMINO'S
STORY

Available now from HarperCollins Leadership

INTRODUCTION

The story of Domino's Pizza is a true rags-to-riches tale, full
of determination, innovation, and ambition. It involves a
long-term vision for a business that would become a global corporate leader, creating jobs and supporting the local economy.
In the present day, it includes a creative, technologically adept
team committed to building a successful enterprise that has
risen to the top of the charts for its industry.

The story begins with Thomas Stephen Monaghan, first son
of Frank and Anna Monaghan, born in 1937. To understand
how Domino's was founded and built, you first have to understand Tom Monaghan's upbringing and early experiences, because they shaped his goals and mind. A self-described
"exuberant" child, full of energy, Monaghan's earliest memories
are of life in Ann Arbor, with his brother, Jim, two years his jun-
ior; a patient, loving father; and a mother who was a good bit
less patient, he relates in *Living the Faith*, a biography of his life.

What shaped his life perhaps more than anything else was the
sudden death of his twenty-nine-year-old doting dad to peritoni-
tis, due to ulcers. Even after a lump-sum payment from Frank's
life insurance policy, Monaghan's mother could barely make
ends meet. She moved her boys into town and got a job at the
Argus Camera Company, but with weekly earnings of $27.50 and
expenses of $30, she knew she had to find a better solution.

That solution was to put her sons into a foster home. They first stayed briefly with one family before being moved for a two-year stint with the Woppmans. However, when Monaghan was around seven, the Woppmans decided he was just too much for them, and returned both boys to their mother.

Around that same time, Anna Monaghan decided to go back to school to become a nurse. Her plan was to place the boys in Catholic boarding school until she earned her degree, and then they would come live with her again when she was making enough money to afford their care. In the meantime, Tom and Jim Monaghan went to live and study at St. Joseph's Home for Boys, which was both a school and an orphanage.

Although he was "intensely unhappy about my strange new surroundings," he says, the light in the darkness was one nun who was uplifting. "Sister Berarda always encouraged me, even when my ideas seemed far-fetched," he says in the book. That included when he told his second-grade class that he was going to be a priest, an architect, *and* shortstop for the Detroit Tigers. Although his classmates laughed, Sister Berarda assured him, "I don't think it's ever been done before, Tommy, but if you want to, there's no reason you can't." And with that, it's likely Monaghan decided he would do just that.

On reflecting on her influence, Monaghan acknowledged how important that relationship had been. "She became my surrogate mother, and I flourished under her care." His own mother worked at the hospital a few blocks away and had an apartment close by, so the boys often visited on weekends, Monaghan recalls. While he excelled in second grade with Sister Berarda's support, when he and Jim were transferred to the local Catholic school in third grade, things took a turn for the worse. The environment was harsh, with whippings common for the smallest infraction, he says, and his grades and attitude fell during his time there. Yet, during those four years, he also says he learned the value of hard work and of not giving up. "If something doesn't work, you try another way. You can't fail." Those teachings certainly served Monaghan well later at Domino's.

Back Together

Finally, when Monaghan was in sixth grade, Anna Monaghan took the boys from St. Joseph's and moved north to Traverse City, Michigan, where she had a job and had bought a house. Suddenly, Monaghan had more freedom than he'd ever experienced, since his mother worked long hours at the hospital. In seventh grade, he enrolled at Immaculate Conception Catholic school and then spent his summer working to earn money through odd jobs. He had already figured out that money was critical to having more freedom, so he sold papers downtown and then vegetables door-to-door to earn some cash.

But after returning from a visit to Monaghan's aunt and uncle's place in Ann Arbor that summer, Anna decided she just couldn't handle him anymore, so she once again placed her sons in foster care. In and out of a few families, when Monaghan began ninth grade at St. Francis High School, he was sent to live on a farm and his brother went back to live with their mother. One of Monaghan's jobs on the farm netted him a paycheck of $2 a week, which he was thrilled about. The house was drafty and he did his homework in the kitchen by the light of a kerosene lamp, then spent his free time reading catalogs, dreaming of the day that he would be able to afford the best of everything. He was going to be rich and famous, he told his friends. And they believed him.

However, he soon had a revelation, due in part to his desire to return to the rituals and routine he had become accustomed to at school. In his freshman year, he says in his book, "I saw that I had been wallowing in crass, worldly thoughts when I should have been concentrating on my spiritual quest. I decided then and there that I would become a priest."

With help, he applied to St. Joseph's Seminary in Grand Rapids, Michigan, and was accepted. He was thrilled, but he only lasted a year there, not due to poor conduct, but because his mother complained to the rector that he wasn't writing home enough. He admits that he didn't write to her as often as other kids wrote to their mothers, but he never would have thought that would get him kicked out of seminary. He was devastated at being asked to leave, and Anna was shocked that her letter had brought him back to her. She hadn't bargained on that.

After another stint in a foster home, Anna had him remanded to a juvenile detention center, until Monaghan's aunt found out and effectively bailed him out, bringing him home with her to Ann Arbor. He says his time with them was the first time since his father's death that he was leading a normal life.

Although he was known for having "grandiose ideas," Monaghan was not invested in his schoolwork. He was more interested in working at local jobs, where he challenged himself to be the best at whatever role he was playing: soda jerk, bowling pin setter, or busboy. Because of his low grades, he didn't bother applying to college, choosing instead to get an apartment and work at a newspaper distributor. Once he had saved up enough money, he applied to the newly opened Ferris State College and was admitted. After his freshman year, his grades were good enough to be admitted to the University of Michigan. But he had no money for tuition, so he joined the military, where he was assigned to the Marine Corps. During his time in the service, he read self-improvement books voraciously.

After being honorably discharged, he went back to Ann Arbor and again got a job with the newspaper distributor. Only this time, the owner taught him the business and Monaghan proved skilled at working with the carriers. He saved his money and finally had enough to enroll at the University of Michigan but soon left after realizing he was in over his head in most of the subjects.

This is why when his mail carrier and part-time pizza delivery-person brother Jim suggested that the two should buy a pizzeria named DomiNick's from its owner, Dominick DiVarti, Tom was game. In fact, he was more than game. He was all in. He saw the potential that the business had to become the start of his business empire—an empire that would eventually allow him to buy the Detroit Tigers. Monaghan wasn't wrong.

As you'll read in the following chapters, through hard work, curiosity, investment in technology, and a focus on customer satisfaction, Monaghan built a business that is still thriving and growing today, more than sixty years later. But Monaghan wasn't just in the right place at the right time. He applied common sense and sound business practices—practices you'll read about and have the opportunity to apply to your own organizations—to establish and grow a global enterprise.

The future is within reach.

When you start making your goals a top priority, everything falls into place. Learn from the leaders inspiring millions & apply their strategies to your professional journey.

*Leadership
Essentials
Blog*

*Activate 180
Podcast*

*Interactive
E-courses*

Free templates

Sign up for our free book summaries!
Inspire your next head-turning idea.
hcleadershipessentials.com/pages/book-summaries

LEADERSHIP
ESSENTIALS
by HarperCollins Leadership

For more business and leadership advice and resources, visit hcleadershipessentials.com.